BLACK POWER 50

Edited by **Sylviane A. Diouf** and **Komozi Woodard**

THE NEW PRESS

NEW YORK
LONDON

Furthermore:
a program of the J.M. Kaplan Fund

This book is made possible with support from Furthermore: a program of the J.M. Kaplan Fund.

Published in the United States by The New Press, New York, 2016
Distributed by Perseus Distribution

ISBN 978-1-62097-148-2 (pbk)
CIP data is available

The New Press publishes books that promote and enrich public discussion and understanding of the issues vital to our democracy and to a more equitable world. These books are made possible by the enthusiasm of our readers; the support of a committed group of donors, large and small; the collaboration of our many partners in the independent media and the not-for-profit sector; booksellers, who often hand-sell New Press books; librarians; and above all by our authors.

www.thenewpress.com

Cover design by C Studio
Interior design by Christina Newhard
This book was set in Mercury and Gotham

Printed in the United States of America

10 9 8 7 6 5 4 3 2 1

CONTENTS

iv / FOREWORD
Khalil Gibran Muhammad

vii / INTRODUCTION
Sylviane A. Diouf and Komozi Woodard

1 / CHAPTER 1
The Black Power Movement, Peniel E. Joseph
Testimonies: Emory Douglas and Maulana Karenga

29 / CHAPTER 2
The Black Power Movement, the Black Panther Party, and
Racial Coalitions, Jakobi Williams
Testimonies: Jose (Cha Cha) Jimenez and Michael James

51 / CHAPTER 3
Black Power and "Education for Liberation," Russell Rickford
Testimony: Ericka Huggins

71 / CHAPTER 4
America Means Prison: Political Prisoners in the Age of Black
Power, Dan Berger
Testimony: Muhammad Ahmad

89 / CHAPTER 5
The Black Arts Movement, James Smethurst

103 / CHAPTER 6
International Dimensions of the Black Power Movement,
Brenda Gayle Plummer
Testimonies: Kathleen Neal Cleaver and Sami Shalom Chetrit

125 / CHAPTER 7
Black Power: The Looks, Jeffrey O. G. Ogbar

137 / CONTRIBUTOR BIOGRAPHIES

140 / NOTES

Foreword

Khalil Gibran Muhammad

Anniversaries are often moments of celebration. These are frequently times to reflect on the difficulties of the past in light of the great progress of the present. As the repository of record for the global black experience, the Schomburg Center for Research in Black Culture has had an outsized role in keeping track of black milestones for nearly a century. Where society erases, teachers are silent, and each generation is prone to forget, we have kept the light of memory alive.

Just three years ago, the Schomburg Center mounted back-to-back exhibitions to commemorate the 150th anniversary of the Emancipation Proclamation, a moment to take stock of the courage of so many unheralded black women and men who transformed this nation. By the measure of the journey from slavery to freedom or, as many noted, the arc of progress from the presidencies of Abraham Lincoln to Barack Obama, there was much to celebrate. And thousands of children and adults visited the center to do exactly that.

But this year, 2016, marks a troubling moment of commemoration. It is the fiftieth anniversary of the dawn of the Black Power era, which was defined by an explosion of radical visions of political, economic, and cultural change among young people beginning in 1966. Inspired by Malcolm X's jeremiads against America's treatment of black people and anti-colonial victories in Africa and Latin America, Black Power activists critiqued the failures of the southern civil rights movement

to extinguish white supremacist ideology and state-sanctioned violence. They redefined Black America as an internal colony and chose their weapons: self-determination, community control, a prideful African-centered identity, and an ethos of communalism. In their politics and in their art, they uncompromisingly asserted the beauty, sanctity, and strength of black life.

Looking back fifty years later, we are supposed to be celebrating their accomplishments. Instead we are bracing for the next uprising. What happened in Watts in 1965, another catalyst for the Black Power era, turns out not to be the past but rather the prologue to what happened in Baltimore in 2015.

When *Black Power 50* was conceived some time ago, first as an exhibition and then as a book, there was no Black Lives Matter movement. State violence by police against unarmed black people had not yet reached a tipping point in firing the conscience of a new generation of young activists. The Voting Rights Act of 1965 was still whole and enforceable. New voter suppression laws aimed at African American and Latino voters had not yet posed a fundamental threat to American democracy and spurred the Moral Mondays movement in North Carolina and elsewhere. Sustained disappointment with the uneven recovery from the Great Recession, with joblessness rates remaining unconscionably high for too many workers and especially young people of color, had not yet led to calls for a Third Reconstruction and the Fight for $15. And no one could have anticipated that Donald Trump's racist, anti-Muslim, nativist, and misogynistic campaign would make him the leading contender for the Republican presidential nomination.

In other words, *Black Power 50* was never meant to be a blueprint for the future. It was never meant to be a source of inspiration for activists today, looking to learn precisely what worked and what didn't from the past.

But this is exactly what you will find in these pages: the dynamic and intensely debated relationships of art to activism, of Marxism to black nationalism, of the local to the international, of black organizing to Chicano, white, and Indian Power. Today's hashtag activists and hunger strikers on university campuses are borrowing strategies from the playbook of black studies founders from the late 1960s. At Princeton University, the University of Missouri, and many other schools, students are occupying the same spaces and buildings that Black Power activists did so many decades before. And their calls for more black and brown students and faculty, more black-centered curricula, and more inclusive campuses exorcised of their slaveholding pasts are little different than before.

When Malcolm X said that "America means prison," as Dan Berger observes, he not only diagnosed the crisis of incarceration for his generation, but he predicted a future where there would be no contradiction in the world's first modern democracy and the greatest prison nation the world has ever known.

Some things have changed for the better, building on the traditions of Ericka Huggins and Kathleen Cleaver. Women activists today have moved to the center of organizing.

Intersectionality as a mode of analysis and activism means no black or brown or poor bodies will be left behind or hidden in the shadows. Queer organizing makes visible all forms of sexuality and oppression simultaneously.

Perhaps the centennial of the Black Power era, fifty years from now, will be a time of celebration and will bring some of the same closure that accompanied the recent anniversary of the end of the Civil War. Until then, we invite you to revisit this past in order to remake the future.

Introduction

Sylviane A. Diouf and Komozi Woodard

June 1966, Greenwood, Mississippi: Stokely Carmichael of the Student Nonviolent Coordinating Committee (SNCC) introduced "Black Power" as a slogan. His fellow SNCC organizer, Willie Ricks, had tested the phrase at rallies earlier. Like no other ideology before, the heterogeneous and ideologically diverse movement that gave the powerful rallying cry its strength and depth shaped black consciousness and built an immense legacy that continues to resonate in the contemporary American landscape. If the exact chronology of the movement is controversial, it is clear that a decade of struggle, including the ferocious repression against it, has had a tremendous impact on issues of not only race and citizenship in the United States but also identity, politics, criminal justice, culture, art, and education globally. Indeed, Black Power's successes and weaknesses have largely molded the past half century.

The year 2016 marks the fiftieth anniversary of Black Power, one of the least understood and most criminalized and vilified movements in American history. Too often presented or remembered primarily as the violent, villainous urban northern counterpoint to the nonviolent, virtuous rural southern civil rights movement, the Black Power movement has been eclipsed in the general public's memory. That blinding binary is an obstacle to our understanding of a more complicated past. Recent scholarship suggests that the civil rights movement in the Jim Crow North preceded the one in the Jim Crow South; and that Black Power

Photographers at a Black Panther rally, Oakland, 1968. Bob Fitch Photography Archive, © Stanford University Libraries, Department of Special Collections.

emerged in the Jim Crow South simultaneously with its ascent in the Jim Crow North and the Jim Crow West. But everywhere, young adults and teenagers led the Black Power movement. Whether they were in Boston, Chicago, or Los Angeles the activists were often the sons and daughters of southern migrants or Caribbean immigrants. Between 1966 and 1976, they developed countless cultural, political, social, and economic programs under the banner of the Black Power ideology. Those programs and organizations, and the art, literature, drama, and music they created, galvanized millions of people in the broadest movement in African American history.

This new generation had become impatient with the civil rights' leadership and limited goals. They were suspicious of official declarations and legislation that suggested an official end to segregation, when they could see that the walls of employment, housing, and school segregation were becoming newly fortified from New York to California. Indeed, the 1964 Civil Rights Act specifically excluded any attack of segregation in the Jim Crow North. Thus, a heated debate developed in the civil rights movement between leaders who declared the struggle for desegregation was over and those who argued it had to continue. Even Dr. Martin Luther King Jr. was attacked by the more conservative leadership, including Roy Wilkins of the National Association for the Advancement of Colored People, who insisted the time for protest was over after the 1965 Voting Rights Act.

Of course, the movement, just like the concept of Black Power itself, was never monolithic. Black Power was heterogeneous, fusing together a number of ideologies and programs, including not only cultural nationalism, socialism, Marxism, and Islam, but also revolutionary nationalism, welfare rights, tenant rights, student voices, revolutionary union movements, Pan-Africanism and so forth—not to mention the rise of black elected officials. The crowded field of organizations included a bewildering spectrum of groups as diverse as SNCC, the Republic of New Afrika (RNA), the Revolutionary Action Movement (RAM), the National Welfare Rights Organization (NWRO), the Black Panther Party (BPP), the African Liberation Support Committee (ALSC), Us Organization, the Congress of African People (CAP), Third World Women Alliance (TWWA), the Organization of Afro-American Unity (OAAU), the Young Lords Organization (YLO), the Black Students Unions (BSU), and the Black Arts Movement (BAM). All of those voices came under the Black Power umbrella.

If Black Power was heterogeneous, it was also fluid. Some activists moved from one organization to the other or belonged to several at the same time. Stokely Carmichael and H. Rap Brown were members of SNCC before joining the Panthers. Carmichael then moved on to the All African People's Revolutionary Party, influenced by Kwame Nkrumah, the deposed former president of Ghana. Muhammad Ahmad, a co-founder of the Revolutionary Action Movement, was also a founder of the African Liberation Support Committee and the African Peoples Party (APP). Robert Williams, formerly of the NAACP, and Queen Mother Moore, once a Communist Party member, were leaders of the Republic of New Afrika and RAM. Some activists belonged to the BPP and the Young Lords. Japanese American Richard Aoki, a field marshal for the BPP, was also the spokesperson for the Asian American Political Alliance (though recent evidence suggests he might have worked for the FBI).

Despite their diversity and, for some, antagonism, all Black Power organizations shared a few fundamental features: they saw themselves as heirs of Malcolm X, defined Black America as an internal colony of the United States, and demanded self-determination. The awareness of forming a "black nationality," a nation within a nation, and of being subjected to systemic racism, became central to the vibrant, self-confident expression of the new black urban experience that marked the era.

While the movement organized countless peaceful demonstrations, the exacerbation of racial conflicts and police brutality led also to increasingly violent confrontations. In the early 1960s, over 320 major rebellions erupted in 257 cities. Following Dr. Martin Luther King's assassination on April 4, 1968, 200 uprisings shook 172 cities. A year later, 500 racial clashes electrified young people,

"FROM GREAT BRITAIN TO THE CARIBBEAN AND FROM INDIA TO ISRAEL, COLONIZED OR MARGINALIZED YOUNG PEOPLE RALLIED AROUND SLOGANS FASHIONED AFTER 'BLACK POWER,' AND ORGANIZATIONS WERE MODELED OR NAMED AFTER THE BLACK PANTHER PARTY."

reshaping black consciousness and reinforcing the quest for autonomy.

In line with Malcolm X's emphasis on the model of the 1955 Bandung Conference that united African and Asian newly independent countries, Black Power also inspired a "Bandung West" of antiracist movements organized by communities of Puerto Ricans, American Indians, Chicanos, Asian Americans, and impoverished working-class whites. Coalitions beyond race, ethnicity, geography, and social origin emerged to fight injustice, discrimination, and economic inequality. Organizations supported each other's struggles, and together their members and sympathizers attended rallies to demand the release of political prisoners. In Chicago, under the leadership of Illinois Black Panther Party deputy chairman Fred Hampton, black, Puerto Rican, and white activists founded the Rainbow Coalition. The 1970 Revolutionary People's Constitutional Convention organized by the BPP in Philadelphia gathered ten thousand to fifteen thousand people with, among others, delegates from the American Indian Movement, the Chicano Brown Berets, the Puerto Rican Young Lords, the Asian American I Wor Kuen, and the mostly white Students for a Democratic Society. Similarly, in the Newark Black Power experiment, the United Brothers—who wanted to achieve Black Power through the electoral process—and the Young Lords signed a mutual defense pact against white terror. They joined together in the 1969 Black and Puerto Rican Political Convention, running candidates on a Rainbow political slate. Los Angeles SNCC's Ralph Featherstone and Us's Maulana Karenga established an alliance at the *Alianza* summit in Albuquerque, New Mexico, with Chicano leader Reies Lopez Tijerina and Hopi chief Tomas Ben Yacya.

In addition to unifying various segments of the American population, the Black Power movement also resonated abroad. Black Power became a global phenomenon, capturing the imagination of anticolonial and other freedom struggles. From Great Britain to the Caribbean and from India to Israel, colonized or marginalized young people rallied around slogans fashioned after "Black Power," and organizations were modeled or named after the Black Panther Party. Young Samoans, Tongans, Cook Islanders, and Maoris founded the Polynesian Panther Movement in New Zealand in 1971, which later became the

Polynesian Panther Party. In Israel, Mizrahi, mostly immigrant Jews from the Middle East and North Africa, called themselves Black Panthers and demanded equality with the European Jews. Dalits, who belong to the lower echelon of society and are outside of the rigid Indian caste system, formed the Dalit Panthers in Bombay. Globally, where youth were denied full citizenship or where governments questioned their very humanity, activists claimed the language of Black Power in the fight for their human rights. Ironically, this suggests the rarely understood paradox that ultimately Black Power was not racial but rather a movement *against* racism.

The radicals in the Black Power movement believed that their antiwar, anticolonial, anti-imperialist, revolutionary stance made the movement a natural ally of the countries that were part of the Soviet bloc during the Cold War: Cuba, Vietnam, China, Ghana, North Korea, Algeria, Tanzania, and Guinea; and of the liberation movements of the Portuguese colonies of Africa as well as of South-West Africa (Namibia) and Rhodesia (Zimbabwe). Whereas few African Americans had actively supported or even been aware of the decolonization movement in Africa in the early 1960s, by 1970 the efforts by Black Power nationalists to support African

divided even further and another layer of discord was added to the mix—one between the African and Caribbean states and the nonstate liberation movements.

Dramatic and rapid political changes in the black world were pushing the movement to the left. The Portuguese colonial empire in Africa—Cape Verde, Guinea-Bissau, Mozambique, and Angola—collapsed under the double assault of the African liberation movements and the 1974 Portuguese "Carnation Revolution." This outcome, added to the defeat of the United States in Vietnam, Laos, and Cambodia, appeared to some American radicals to indicate that revolution was imminent in the United States. The delusion that "revolution was just around the corner" was a fatal mistake. Divisive attempts to form a Russian-style revolutionary party led a number of Black Power groups to demobilize or unravel key national organizations—including the Congress of African People—that controlled vital links in a national political and communications infrastructure. In addition, the Russian reputation for secret cadres made it even easier for police groups and agent provocateurs to stir conflict and cause unnecessary strife. Mutual trust was an invaluable asset to the youthful Black Power movement, but by 1976 that asset was replaced by widespread mutual distrust. At a few New York political rallies, activists fought each other with baseball bats. Howard Fuller and his allies were kidnapped and tortured by rival factions in a new "Revolutionary Wing."

Across the broader movement, signs of unravelling were everywhere. In academia, black studies programs were shaken by ideological debates, and the editors of the *Black Scholar* journal—founded in California in 1969—split into two opposing camps: the cultural nationalists accused the others of favoring a Marxist agenda, which the latter denied. *Black World,* edited by Hoyt Fuller, was shut down by publisher John Johnson in 1975. Some political organizations disappeared overnight. The leaders of the African Liberation Support Committee vacated its national headquarters without notice; the regional and local branches were left in chaos. The National Black Political Assembly, which grew out of the Gary Convention,

exploded into warring camps. In the end, key Black Power militants surrendered leadership, while others were unable to stop the movement's downfall.

—

Despite its divisions and weaknesses, the Black Power movement's influence is still felt today in ways that have become so woven into the national fabric that few recognize them as the legacy of this youth-led movement.

On the cultural front, the Black Arts Movement inspired the creation of some eight hundred black theaters and cultural centers in the country. Writers and artists in dozens of cities, from Newark to San Francisco, New Orleans, Chicago, and Detroit, created alternative institutions. Many disappeared, but some are still in operation, as are Black Arts festivals and journals. The central influence of the Black Power on hip-hop and spoken word artists cannot be overstated. And Kwanzaa has been part of mainstream America for decades.

On the social front, free school breakfasts, first established by the Black Panther Party, were the precursors to the free lunch program that exists throughout the country. Sickle-cell anemia awareness campaigns and testing were also launched by the BPP, which understood health as a basic human right.

One further, crucial legacy of the movement is so prevalent that it is nearly taken for granted. Following in Black Power's footsteps, American Indian, Asian American, Hispanic, LGBT, and women's groups asserted themselves and demanded representation. The politics of group identity—once limited to white straight males—entered mainstream education, academia, culture, politics, and society at large.

To understand recent African American history, and ultimately American society more generally, one must come to terms with the depth and breadth, and the achievements and shortcomings of the Black Power movement.

BLACK POWER 50

The Black Power movement viewed African Americans as a colonized people and linked its struggle to those of other oppressed and marginalized people worldwide. In 1967, James Forman, Student Nonviolent Coordinating Committee's executive secretary and director of its International Affairs Commission, addressed the UN General Assembly, calling African Americans an oppressed nation. Forman later became the minister of foreign affairs of the Black Panther Party. James Baldwin, Joan Baez, and James Forman during a civil rights march. © Dr. Laurance G. Henry Collection. Photographs and Prints Division, Schomburg Center for Research in Black Culture, The New York Public Library.

CHAPTER I

The Black Power Movement

Peniel E. Joseph

The Black Power movement's modern face draws from both the New Negro radicalism of the 1920s and the Great Depression and World War II–era freedom surges—distinct yet overlapping political and historical traditions that indelibly shaped twentieth-century radical black activism. Black Power activists extolled the virtues of radical political self-determination, brokered alliances with third-world revolutionaries, and emphasized racial pride as both a shield against white supremacy and a sword capable of defeating institutional racism, global capitalism, and Western imperialism.

Black Power activists observed, criticized, and participated in the civil rights movement's heroic years. These years, from 1954 to 1965, were marked by bus boycotts, sit-ins, political assassinations, and legal and legislative victories that riveted the national consciousness and have been successfully upheld by contemporary historians as the most important social and political development of the postwar era. The civil rights era has by now become enshrined in America's national memory as a collective moral and political good.

However, Black Power is still too often viewed as a destructive, short-lived, and politically ineffectual movement that triggered white backlash, resulted in urban rioting, and severely crippled the mainstream civil rights struggle. Black Power's classical period (1966–75) is most often characterized as a kind of feverish dream dominated by outsized personalities who spewed words of fire, making this a justly forgotten era. Moreover, histories of the New Left tend to blame Black Power radicalism for inspiring white radicals toward a simplistic and tragically romantic view of "revolutionary" violence.

New scholarship, which I have called "Black Power Studies," is changing the way in which historians, teachers, students, and the general public view Black Power, civil rights, the 1960s, and more generally, postwar American history. Black Power is too often portrayed as a temporary eruption that existed outside the confines of American history; the movement's important antiwar activism, antipoverty efforts, foreign policy interventions, intellectual and political debates, local character, and national influence have been virtually ignored. Black Power studies place this history back within the broader context of American and African American history at the local, national, and international levels.

The roots of the modern Black Power

" THE ROOTS OF THE MODERN BLACK POWER MOVEMENT ARE FOUND IN THE DOMESTIC AND INTERNATIONAL FREEDOM STRUGGLES OF THE GREAT DEPRESSION AND WORLD WAR II ERA. "

Black Power graffiti. Brooklyn, 1971. © Stephen Shames.

movement are found in the domestic and international freedom struggles of the Great Depression and World War II era, a time when coalitions of civil rights activists, trade unionists, liberals, radicals, and pan-Africanists demanded a deeper, more expansive vision of American democracy. Political mobilizers such as performing artist Paul Robeson, labor leader Asa Philip Randolph, New Dealer Mary McLeod Bethune, and the venerable intellectual W.E.B. Du Bois advocated a national movement for racial and economic justice and world peace. Grassroots organizers such as Ella Baker gave the movement local voice, and it took root from Harlem's bleak street corners through the union organizing efforts in Winston-Salem, North Carolina, and interracial antiracist activities in Birmingham, Alabama, to the postwar boomtowns of Oakland and Los Angeles. Cold War repression dramatically scaled back these efforts, which would be replaced, at least at the national level, with a southern civil rights movement that gingerly couched its efforts within the context of Cold War liberalism's pungent anti-Communism.

In 1954, the same year as the Supreme Court's *Brown v. Board of Education* desegregation decision, Malcolm X arrived in Harlem as the head minister of the Nation of Islam's Muslim Mosque No. 7 on West 116th Street.

Over the course of the next decade Malcolm would practice a unique brand of coalition politics that attracted two generations of African American radicals. The older group included veteran street speakers, activists, and radicals who had come of political age during the freedom surge of the 1940s only to be disappointed (and at times criminalized) by the Cold War. The most notable of

these figures included the writer John Oliver Killens and Harlem historian John Henrik Clarke, both leading members of the Harlem Writers Guild. Malcolm also attracted a younger generation of activists, including the poets LeRoi Jones (later Amiri Baraka) and Maya Angelou. Harlem powerbrokers such as Congressman Adam Clayton Powell Jr. and *New York Amsterdam News* editor James

Hicks were among the coterie of influential political, journalistic, and civic figures whom Malcolm counted as allies.

On February 15, 1961, Maya Angelou, Abbey Lincoln, and Rosa Guy, at the helm of the Cultural Association of Women of African Heritage (CAWAH), were joined by many of Harlem's leading activists who viewed Malcolm as their political leader to stage a demonstration at the United Nations Security Council in protest against the murder of Patrice Lumumba, the first prime minister of the Democratic Republic of Congo. In the ensuing melee dozens were arrested. The *New York Times* described it as the "worst day of violence" in the UN's history. Ralph Bunche may have deplored the "hooliganism" of the blacks who "rioted" at the United Nations, but James Baldwin and Lorraine Hansberry sounded a different note, writing to the *Times* to express deep disappointment with stories and rumors that characterized the demonstration as a Communist plot. According to Baldwin and Hansberry, the Lumumba demonstration represented a call for radical democracy that connected anticolonial struggles being waged in Africa with domestic freedom surges engulfing America.

Outside of New York City, Malcolm made deep inroads among organizers in Detroit, where in 1961 local militants such as Reverend Albert Cleage, James and Grace Lee Boggs, and Richard and Milton Henry formed the Group On Advanced Leadership (GOAL), an organization that represented early Black Power impulses. Detroit also housed the militant group UHURU, Swahili for "freedom," taken from Kenya's Mau Mau movement. UHURU featured some of the city's angriest and most youthful militants. On June 23, 1963, political organizers in Detroit associated with Malcolm shared a stage with Martin Luther King during the Motor City's massive "Walk to Freedom," a pro-Birmingham sympathy march that drew 125,000 participants. Five months later, Malcolm delivered the keynote address at the Grassroots Leadership

EMORY DOUGLAS

Love for the Community

Emory Douglas was the minister of culture of the Black Panther Party.

Were you, like many young people involved in the Black Power movement, part of the Second Great Migration of Southerners moving west?

No, I was born in Grand Rapids, Michigan. My mother came to Michigan from Oklahoma. She had a sister in San Francisco. I had asthma as a kid, and the doctors told her that they thought the climate here might be better for me, so that's why we came to San Francisco in 1951.

How did you get involved with the Black Panther Party?

I got involved with the BPP while in the Black Arts Movement where I had created and contributed my own artwork, such as poster art, event announcements, and flyers, along with doing simple stage-prop designs for Amiri Baraka's plays. I also did the cover artwork for Sonia Sanchez's first poetry book, titled *Homecoming*. I was

basically self-taught. I had a limited amount of professional art training at City College of San Francisco where I majored in commercial art and learned the commercial aspect of doing graphic designing for various types of publications, point-of-purchase displays, posters, film animation and all the overall production aspects of graphic design. While I was in the Black Arts Movement, there was the Northern California Black Panther Party based in San Francisco; they were planning an event to bring Betty Shabazz, Malcom X's widow, to the Bay Area to honor her. I was asked by an activist friend to do the poster for that event. During the planning sessions they talked about some guys coming over to the next planning session and let it be known if they would do security for the event, which they did agree to do. That was Huey Newton and Bobby Seale. After I met them I asked how

The Lowndes County Freedom Organization, which became known as the "Black Panther Party," chose a black panther because the animal does not attack, but would not move back. Huey P. Newton and Bobby Seale later used the name and emblem for the Black Panther Party for Self-Defense. © Dr. Laurance G. Henry Collection. Photographs and Prints Division, Schomburg Center for Research in Black Culture, The New York Public Library.

could I join. That became my first introduction and the beginning of my transition into the Black Panther Party, in late January 1967, about three months after the Party started. I was just about twenty-one, going twenty-two. The pioneering members were from sixteen to eighteen, nineteen years of age. I think Huey Newton was twenty-three and Bobby Seale and Elbert "Big Man" Howard were around twenty-eight and thirty.

The newspaper, the Black Panther, is renowned globally because of your art; and fifty years later you're still invited all over the world to show it and talk about it. Were you involved in the paper from the start?

When I joined the BPP the newspaper had not started as yet. Bobby Seale and Elbert "Big Man" Howard, who was the first editor and an original member of the Black Panther Party, put out the first issue

on April 2, 1967. It was a mimeograph paper. It was after that first issue that I began to work on the newspaper. I was the revolutionary artist, it was my first title. In mid-1967, that is when we first started to get titles. And then later I became the minister of culture.

The newspaper looked quite professional.

In the beginning it was just myself and Eldridge Cleaver

and then Kathleen Cleaver, and we used to work out of a studio apartment. But then we developed to the point where I had a cadre of people who worked with me. We had a photography department, we had our typesetters, we had editors. We had those who coordinated the design and lettering and formatting, and we had a darkroom where we developed film and photographs. As we evolved, the quality got better. It was a grassroots paper but as we critiqued and evaluated our work, we improved. Our newspaper national distribution operation was located in San Francisco, where the production work was done to ship the papers to the different chapters and branches and to wherever else they were being requested.

Two years after joining the Party you went to Algeria.

In 1969, I went to Algeria for the first time. Eldridge was in

exile because he didn't want to go back to prison. He went to Cuba and then he was on his way to Algeria. Kathleen worked it out for me to travel with her to Algeria. We went to France first, and we stayed with Julia Wright, Richard Wright's daughter, and her mother Ellen. And from there we went to Algiers. I remember we met Yasser Arafat, who was there for a conference. We had round-tables with all the different African Liberation movements. And we were invited in 1969 to participate in the first Pan-African Cultural Festival where countries from all over Africa were represented.

What was it like to live and work with the Panthers?

As the Party evolved, it became clear what it needed to do in order to stay cohesive and to get the work done was to develop our collective living situation. We knew people who were in real

estate and they helped us rent apartments we shared collectively. Plus, we knew how to hustle the game. When Panthers went to see about renting apartments—but not in uniform—they would tell the building manager, "I work at such and such a place, this is the number." So the landlords or the agents would call the Panther number that we had set up for them to inquire about the rental application details. Of course there was always high praise given. Then you had veteran Panthers who came out of Vietnam into the Party. They got GI loans and could buy houses. We had veterans in the organization across the country who bought houses where we lived collectively.

Education was a crucial part of the Black Panther Party and the Black Power movement in general.

We always had political education classes; we talked about

———

Conference in Detroit, an event that featured key early Black Power activists and culminated in an effort to build a national movement for black self-determination.

In Ohio in 1962, militant black college students formed the Revolutionary Action Movement (RAM), a group that anticipated the Black Panther Party's call for armed self-defense and viewed Malcolm X and Robert F. Williams as the leaders of a radical movement for African American liberation. This loose coalition of militants included journalist William Worthy, who founded the Freedom Now Party in 1963 and formed a political relationship with Malcolm X and Dan Watts, the publisher of the radical monthly magazine *Liberator,* which documented the relationship between the Third World and domestic civil rights struggles.

In short, from 1954 up until his death in 1965, Malcolm X led a movement for Black Power that paralleled and intersected with the civil rights movement's high tide. Conventional civil rights historiography largely ignores this story. Instead, it begins its coverage of Black Power in June 1966,

world history and domestic issues. There were required readings in the Party. Even though people weren't on the same level, you had to put the effort in, read the newspaper, discuss what was in it, critique and evaluate our work and responsibilities. How to improve the quality of work; all those things were always a part of the learning process. And that became consistent all across the country. The chapters and branches that wanted to start had to come out to the base here in California to see how things were run. There was a structure. They were required to sell newspapers and help with education classes.

The Panthers' community work is often overlooked.

There was a time when we were in uniforms, and there were all these shootouts happening and we were thinking we were going to start a revolution. But the people are not rising up. It's the Black Panthers being shot and the people on the sideline saying, "Right-on Black Panthers," but they're not getting involved en masse. So it was time for us to take off the uniform and get into the community and begin doing some real serious organizing. It was like, "Put down the books, now you know all the theory; go out there and put it into practice." We went to merge with the community, to serve the interests and needs of the community and to be an inspiration. We also educated and enlightened people about their government's misdeeds. And that's how you have all these alternative institutions and schools. People were really interested in that and it became the real thorn in the side of the government, because now we're beginning to transform the mindsets of people about what the government should have

been doing to help people in need and by so doing we became the government's public enemy number one.

What is the Panthers' legacy?

The Party's legacy is that we left a blueprint not to duplicate but to be inspired by: our social programs, genuine love for the community, and our self-determination for basic human rights.

— *Interview by Sylviane A. Diouf*

TOP: Huey P. Newton and Bobby Seale co-founded the Black Panther Party for Self-Defense in October 1966. The Party's earliest political thinking was rooted in "revolutionary nationalism," a combination of black nationalism and anticolonialism. Oakland, 1972. © Stephen Shames. LEFT: SNCC activists Stokely Carmichael and H. Rap Brown embrace after Carmichael's release from prison in Prattville, Alabama, in June 1967. Jim Peppler/Southern Courier Photograph Collection/Alabama Department of Archives and History, Montgomery, Alabama. RIGHT: With twelve thousand delegates, the March 1972 National Black Political Convention in Gary, Indiana, was perhaps the zenith of Black Power politics. Delegates drafted a fifty-five-page document, the National Black Agenda, which challenged the white establishment monopoly on American political discourse. © Chester Higgins Jr./chesterhiggins.com. All rights reserved.

> ## " BLACK POWER IS NOT USUALLY ASSOCIATED WITH WELFARE, TENANT-RIGHTS ACTIVISM, AND ANTIPOVERTY EFFORTS, YET THE MOVEMENT MADE THESE ISSUES SOME OF ITS CORE PRIORITIES. "

with Stokely Carmichael's fiery declaration on a humid Thursday evening in Greenwood, Mississippi. Yet even the Black Power era's classical period has received inadequate attention by professional historians.

Black Power grew out of the political, economic, and racial reality of postwar America, when the possibilities of American democracy seemed unlimited. Black Power activists challenged American hegemony at home and abroad, demanded full citizenship, and vociferously criticized political reforms that at times substituted tokenism and style over substance. Some activists did this through a sometimes bellicose advocacy of racial separatism contoured by threats of civil unrest. Others sought equal access to predominantly white institutions, especially public schools, colleges, and universities, while many decided to build independent, black-led institutions designed to serve as new beacons for African American intellectual achievement, political power, and cultural pride. Yet such efforts did not exist in a vacuum. Organized black activists encountered political repression at the local, national, and international levels. A complex web of criminal justice and police agencies infiltrated, harassed, and helped to eventually cripple Black Power's most visibly militant groups.

Black Power is not usually associated with welfare, tenant-rights activism, and antipoverty efforts, yet the movement made these issues some of its core priorities. The National Welfare Rights Organization, which represented a far-flung series of local welfare rights chapters and organizations, stands out as one of the most important Black Power groups of the 1960s and early 1970s. Activists in such cities as Baltimore, Philadelphia, New Orleans, Newark, Los Angeles, and Las Vegas used the movement's insurgent rhetoric, bold strategies, and defiant tactics to push for bread-and-butter issues, especially those impacting poor black women heading single-family households.

The movement advocated radical goals that were tempered by an at times surprising and effective blend of militancy and pragmatism. Organized protests for Black Studies, efforts to incorporate the Black Arts Movement into independent and existing institutions, and the thrust to take control of major American cities through electoral strength exemplified these impulses. Black Power activism's influence stretched from prisons to trade unions to local and national political elections. Internationally, Black Power militants forged alliances with iconic Third World leaders including Fidel Castro, Mao Tse-tung, Kwame Nkrumah, Sékou Touré, Amilcar Cabral, Nelson Mandela, Mohammad Babu,

Maulana Karenga (center) founded the cultural nationalist organization Us in 1965. Karenga wrote a doctrine which he called Kawaida, meaning "tradition and reason." Us promoted self-determination and self-reliance and introduced the holiday Kwanzaa. Los Angeles, 1969. © William James Warren/Science Faction/Corbis.

and Julius Nyerere. Leading American political figures of the postwar era, most notably Lyndon Baines Johnson, Hubert Humphrey, Ramsey Clark, Nicholas Katzenbach, Richard Nixon, and J. Edgar Hoover, regarded the movement as dangerous, unpredictable, and a threat to national security. Yet the movement's impact on American history, its successes, failures, and shortcomings as well as it contemporary legacy, remain undervalued and understudied.

The historiography of the modern civil rights movement generally views Black Power as a movement composed of armed urban militants inspired more by rage than an actual political program. The Black Panther Party for Self-Defense (BPP), a group of young black men and women from California's Bay Area, has come to personify the period in the

LEFT: Amiri Baraka became the general-secretary of the National Black Political Assembly that grew out of the 1972 Gary Convention. Left to right: Congress of African People chair, Amiri Baraka; Detroit, Michigan, U.S. representative and Black Congressional Caucus chair Charles Diggs; and Gary, Indiana, mayor Richard Hatcher at Gary Convention press conference. © Risasi Zachariah Dais. RIGHT: Saidi Nguvu of the Newark Congress of African People; Stokely Carmichael/Kwame Ture and Cleveland Sellers of the All African People's Revolutionary Party. Ture and Sellers were veterans of SNCC. © Risasi Zachariah Dais.

historical imagination. The Black Panthers are most often remembered for their bold public persona—replete with leather jackets, tilted berets, and guns—than for their ten-point program, which called for the fundamental transformation of black poverty in central

DR. MAULANA KARENGA

Black Power, Black Liberation, and Us: A Reflective Remembering and Recounting

The Black Power movement and our organization Us emerge at a critical juncture in the history of our people, this country, and the world. It is a time of fundamental turning defined and shaped by several interrelated factors including: 1) the historical exhaustion of the civil rights period of the Black Freedom movement and the emergence of its Black Power period; 2) the assassination and martyrdom of Min. Malcolm X and the embrace of his legacy by Us and other nationalist groups; 3) the Watts rebellion and subsequent revolts

and other forms of resistance across the United States; and 4) the liberation struggles of continental Africans and other peoples of the Third World.

Malcolm X noted in *Malcolm X Speaks* that "We are living in an era of revolution and revolt, and the (African American) is a part of the rebellion against oppression and colonialism which has characterized this era." Thus, Us is conceived and constructed in the crucible of struggle, both political and ideological, and when I called together a cadre of men and women to my house

to found Us, September 7, 1965, we were well aware of and eager to engage in these critical struggles. We saw ourselves as the ideological sons and daughters of Malcolm, veterans of the Watts rebellion, and heirs of a long legacy of struggle. We were new soldiers and warriors who would carry the struggle forward in honor of our ancestors, in the interests of our people, and in cooperative advancement of the liberation of the world from racism and white supremacy in its various forms.

We called our organization

Us, i.e., us Black people, African people. It was a name chosen to declare commitment to all of us, all of our people, everywhere; to stress the collective and cooperative character of our philosophy, practice, and project; and to express and maintain a clear distinction between us and "them," the oppressor, on every vital and necessary level. Moreover, we declared ourselves a revolutionary vanguard, committed to our people and to our liberation struggle. Clearly, Us's signature, most widespread, and most known achievements are the pan-African institution of Kwanzaa and the black value system of *Nguzo Saba,* the Seven Principles: *Umoja* (unity), *Kujichagulia* (self-determination), *Ujima* (collective work and responsibility), *Ujamaa* (cooperative economics), *Nia* (purpose), *Kuumba* (creativity), and *Imani* (faith). And although it is not as well known, *Kawaida* philosophy is not only the intellectual anchor and animating philosophy of these institutions, but the foundation and framework for all of Us's work, struggle, and achievement. Indeed, both Kwanzaa and the Nguzo Saba are creative and intellectual products of Kawaida, which is defined as an ongoing synthesis of the best of African thought and practice in constant exchange with the world.

Part of Us's uniqueness and importance lies in its role as the founding organization of Kwanzaa, celebrated by millions throughout the world African community and which I created in 1966. Kwanzaa is a communal practice that stresses and reaffirms Africanness and binds Black people together in ways unlike any other institution or celebration. The Nguzo Saba, at the heart of Kwanzaa, are not only central to its practice, but also serve as philosophical grounding and a guide to daily living for millions of African people throughout the global African community and thousands of organizations representing a wide range of educational, political, social, economic, and cultural formations. Indeed, no other organization or philosophy from the 1960s has had such a similar widespread programmatic and philosophical impact on African organizational, family, and personal life.

We defined Black Power as the collective struggle of our people to achieve three overarching and yet basic goals: self-determination, self-respect, and self-defense. Self-determination called for control of the space we occupied, the end of internal colonialism, liberation from oppression in all forms, and freedom to realize our potential and flourish as persons and a people. Self-respect called for a rootedness in the best of our cities. The BPP's organizational history offers a window into the era's political and ideological diversity. The group's earliest political thinking was rooted in "revolutionary nationalism," a combination of black nationalism and anticolonialism that gained momentum in the early 1960s through not only the CAWAH United Nations protest but also the cultural criticism of writer Harold Cruse and the political activism of Robert F. Williams.

The BPP's co-founders, Huey P. Newton and Bobby Seale, adopted an interpretation of revolutionary nationalism that they were introduced to via the Revolutionary Action Movement (RAM), a group that included Muhammad Ahmad (Max Stanford) and Donald Freedman and came to be considered a forerunner to Black Power–era groups of the late 1960s. RAM admired Malcolm X and Williams, formed alliances with Detroit radicals James and Grace Lee Boggs, and helped publish *Soulbook,* an influential political magazine whose staff included Bobby Seale and Ernie Allen.

The organizational genealogy that produced the Panthers usually ignores the powerful, direct influence of the Lowndes County Freedom Organization (LCFO), which combined local grassroots activism with a call for radical self-determination that proved historic. Student Nonviolent Coordinating Committee (SNCC) activists Stokely Carmichael, Bob Mants, and Judy Richardson in Lowndes County and H. Rap Brown in Greene County joined forces with local sharecroppers and activists to help transform the buckle of Alabama's black belt into the headquarters of a political revolt whose reverberations reached all the way to Oakland, California.

own culture in ways that gave us the consciousness and capacity to be ourselves, free ourselves, and reaffirm our identity, dignity, and humanity. And self-defense called for a defiant assertion of our right and responsibility to protect ourselves and our people, resist oppression, and seek freedom by any and all appropriate and necessary means—armed or otherwise.

Reading and absorbing the writings of the major revolutionaries and liberation leaders of our time, especially Malcolm X, Frantz Fanon, Sékou Touré, Julius Nyerere, Robert Williams, Amilcar Cabral, Marcus Garvey, and others, we stressed cultural revolution, liberation struggle, pan-Africanism, and Third World solidarity. We took Malcolm's teachings that we are a nation within a nation, and we understood our people as a nation, a cultural nation struggling to come into political existence, i.e., struggling to free itself and be itself.

Thus we defined ourselves as Kawaida cultural nationalists, *revolutionary* cultural nationalists, in spite of mischaracterizations and misinformation about Us spread by the FBI and other opponents. Kawaida cultural nationalism is for Us thought and practice rooted in three basic propositions: 1) the defining feature of a people or a nation is its culture; 2) for a people to be itself and free itself, it must be self-determined, self-conscious, and rooted in its own culture; and 3) the quality of life of a people and the success of their liberation struggle depend on their waging *cultural revolution within* and *political revolution without,* resulting in a radical restructuring of self and society and ultimately impacting the world.

We were anticapitalist, advocating African socialism, defined in great part by Mwalimu Nyerere's concept of *Ujamaa.* We taught and practiced draft resistance, cooperatively organized and held antiwar rallies and teach-ins against imperialist wars in Africa, Asia, and Latin America, and supported the right of self-determination for all peoples. We advocated reparations and prisoners' rights, trained *Kasisi* (chaplains) to counsel and advise prisoners, and provided literature and lawyers where possible. As pan-Africanists, we supported African liberation movements and pan-Africanist projects; and we built alliances with various Third World organizations engaging in the struggles that gave rise to and defined the times.

Realizing with other liberation movements that we have to build and sustain the people as we fight, we committed ourselves to work, service, struggle, and institution-building. Thus, we established numerous organizing initiatives and worked in cooperative community projects to build institutions to provide affordable housing, accessible health care, and quality education; end police

In an effort to gain political autonomy, the LCFO ran local candidates for political office, featuring a Black Panther on the ballot—a symbolic repudiation of the Democratic and Republican parties as well as racial terrorists who practiced violent intimidation in an effort to quell black power.

The organization Us (black people, African people) helped raise black consciousness through its promotion of cultural practices, but is most often remembered for a series of violent confrontations with the Black Panthers. Us introduced the black holiday Kwanzaa to the African American community. Founder Maulana Karenga's (formerly Ron Everett) advocacy of a black value system found its most important disciple in Amiri Baraka (LeRoi Jones), who would adopt and revise the Nguzo Saba in Newark through the Committee for a Unified Newark (CFUN) and later the Congress of African People (CAP). For a brief but important time, Us was one of the most important Black Power groups, organizing the National Black Power Conferences and showcasing the way in which black nationalists in Los Angeles utilized culture in an effort to transform the racial and political consciousness of the black community. By 1969, however, Us and the Panthers were engaged in violent and sectarian conflicts

———

Stokely Carmichael/Kwame Ture of the All African People's Revolutionary Party, a Pan-Africanist, socialist party that advocated the revolutionary unity of Africa. Stokely Carmichael, 0227527, Special Collections Research Center, North Carolina State University Libraries, Raleigh, North Carolina.

LEFT: The Black Panthers provided free sickle-cell anemia testing. Oakland, 1972. © Stephen Shames. RIGHT: The Young Lords Party was founded in New York in 1969. It offered free breakfasts and daycare centers for children, and helped bring about changes in public sanitation, improvements in health care facilities, elimination of lead-based paints, and reforms at the Board of Corrections. Co-founder Felipe Luciano (on stage with microphone) introduces the YLP at a meeting in Tompkins Square Park, New York, July 26, 1969. © Hiram Maristany.

abuse and violence; establish economic cooperatives; increase political participation; and expand space for cultural grounding, creativity, and performances. Practicing the Kawaida principle of operational unity, unity in diversity, unity without uniformity, Us initiated and helped build Black united fronts across the country in places such as Los Angeles, Newark, San Diego, and Dayton.

Having been invited to participate in the first Black Power Conference in Washington, D.C., called by Rep. Adam Clayton Powell in 1966, Us played a major role in co-planning, co-hosting and providing ideological grounding for the two subsequent Black Power Conferences in Newark, 1967, and Philadelphia, 1968. At the Newark conference, we were given the assignment of organizing a political campaign to actualize Black Power and chose Newark as the site for the initiative. There we led and organized

a political campaign I called "Peace and Power" and during which I trained and organized political workers and candidates. This initiative involved the building of a Black united front, the Committee for a United Newark (CFUN,) and led to the election of many city councilpersons and Newark's first Black mayor.

Like other organizations of the Black Liberation Movement, Us was initially patriarchal. However, the organization began to change to an egalitarian formation as a result of several interrelated factors. These include: 1) the ongoing dialog on gender relations in which the women of Us began to question and resist established relations; 2) the heightened state of suppression of the organization and an increasing number of male members being imprisoned or going underground or in exile; 3) the emergence of the women in new and expanded administrative, security, and public roles and

accompanying dialog and decisions on mutual respect, equality, and shared responsibility in life, love, and struggle; 4) the changing context of the Movement itself and the need for Us to reaffirm its revolutionary character; and 5) the demand of Kawaida to practice the best of African culture in constant exchange with the world. Representative documents of this dialog and change are the Malaika Women's Statement, "View from the Woman's Side of the Circle," published in Us's paper, *Harambee,* on April 25, 1969, and in articles I wrote in the *Black Scholar* during my political imprisonment, including "A Strategy for Struggle: Turning Weakness into Strength" (1973) and "In Love and Struggle: Toward a Greater Togetherness" (1975).

Although it is routinely omitted in the literature, we, like other Black Power organizations, were victims of the COINTELPRO, the FBI program to "discredit, disrupt

LEFT: White radicals and activists who wanted to work with white youth in poor and working-class neighborhoods of Chicago to help overcome deep-seated racism founded Rising Up Angry. They allied themselves with the Black Panther Party, the Young Lords, and other groups to form the Rainbow Coalition. © Michael James. RIGHT: Deputy chairman and co-founder of the Illinois chapter of the BPP Fred Hampton (center with beret) alongside co-founder and former SNCC member Bobby Rush at a Panther rally in Chicago, 1969. Hampton launched the Rainbow Coalition. During an early morning raid on December 4, 1969, the police assassinated Hampton and fellow Black Panther Mark Clark while they slept and wounded seven other members. © Hiroji Kubota/Magnum Photos.

and destroy and otherwise neutralize" all Black leadership and organizations deemed to be a security threat. Other targets of this program included the Nation of Islam, the Student Nonviolent Coordinating Committee, the Republic of New Afrika, the Black Panther Party, the Revolutionary Action Movement, and the Movement in general. We were on every list any other Black Power group viewed as a threat to the country's security was on. According to FBI files, such a group was considered a revolutionary organization if it was "armed and dangerous," if its leader "plans a revolution, . . . is currently training members in revolutionary tactics and is currently storing arms," and if it is an "organization whose aims include the overthrow of or destruction of the U.S. by unlawful means." And according to another report, the FBI stated it had "information which indicates Us is engaged in activities which could violate"

a series of U.S. Title 18 Codes, including those against: "revolution or insurrection," "seditious conspiracy," and "advocating overthrow of the Government," as well as Title 22 concerning "Neutrality Matters," i.e., dealing with foreign countries deemed enemies.

This led to ongoing surveillance and suppression of Us and its members by the national and local police and security forces, resulting in deaths, shootings, attacks on our homes and headquarters, persistent harassment, and continuing character assassination. Us members were driven underground and into exile, and in some cases, including my own, suffered political imprisonment on trumped-up charges. Also, the FBI was responsible for manipulative propaganda and the provocation of intergroup struggles, especially the deadly shootouts between the Panthers and Us. What Hoover feared, after all, was not any one group,

but rather the unity and coordinated struggle of our groups as a self-conscious revolutionary and transformative social force.

We are simultaneously *victims* and *survivors* of the COINTEL-PRO, refusing to be dispirited, defeated, or diverted from the ongoing struggle to radically restructure society and contribute meaningfully to a new history and hope for Africans and humankind. In September 2015, Us advocates/members celebrated the fiftieth anniversary of the organization and the Nguzo Saba, and by extension Kawaida, the philosophy and value system used by millions of Africans throughout the world African community to ground themselves, do their work, and to orient, enrich, and expand their lives.

Us has continued to play a unique and vanguard role in Black intellectual, creative, and political culture since the 1960s, including Black Arts, Black

that were based on ideological disputes, personal grudges, and youthful ego, tensions that were exploited by the FBI's illegal COINTELPRO Program, which attempted to destroy black radicalism through harassment, surveillance, and sometimes violence.

Us also illustrates the close and overlapping organizational histories of the era.

———

Members of the Brown Berets, a Chicano organization founded by David Sanchez, an East Los Angeles high school student, in 1967. The Brown Berets had close to ninety chapters in the West and the Southwest, as well as in Michigan and Minnesota, and about five thousand members total. Reies Lopez Tijerina (center) crusaded for land grants for Chicanos in New Mexico, as the Republic of New Afrika did for African Americans in the South. Oakland, 1968. Bob Fitch Photography Archive, © Stanford University Libraries, Department of Special Collections.

Karenga belonged to the Los Angeles chapter of the Afro-American Association, a Bay Area black consciousness-raising group that included Bobby Seale and Huey P. Newton. Like Newton and Seale, Karenga considered himself a disciple of the slain black icon, Malcolm X. Karenga presided over the Black Congress, an early effort at organizational solidarity, including Elaine Brown and the BPP. The Black Congress helped to coordinate California's Black Power organizations, mediate disputes, and was an early supporter of efforts to free Black Panther minister of defense Huey P. Newton. Also, in an event that attracted 6,500 people, Karenga hosted keynote speaker Stokely Carmichael one year after the Watts rebellion.

Stokely Carmichael (later Kwame Ture) is usually dismissed as a temperamental

rabble-rouser who helped to subvert more promising movements for social justice. Yet such a characterization ignores Carmichael's civil rights activism in the Deep South between 1960 and 1966, where he suffered physical violence and racial terror in pursuit of radical democracy. Carmichael's willingness to endure personal sacrifice and years of struggle for democratic principles that upheld black sharecroppers as symbols of a new American egalitarianism complicates old narratives of the Black Power era. Carmichael's political evolution took place within SNCC, the most important grassroots civil rights/Black Power–era organization.

SNCC housed competing political ideologies, including liberal integrationism, black nationalism, feminism, and anti-imperialism. By 1966 SNCC's dreams of interracial democracy had been transformed by traumatic and tragic experience. The group issued a stinging denunciation against the Vietnam War, a manifesto that placed the organization at the cutting edge of a Black Power–led anti-imperialist movement that would soon include the Black Panthers, Students for a Democratic Society, and the New Left. In 1970 SNCC activists Frances Beal and Gwen Patton organized the Third World's Women Alliance (TWWA), which grew out of SNCC's Black Women's Liberation Committee. A daring combination of radical black feminism, socialism, and Black Power–era militancy, TWWA organized black and Puerto Rican feminists in consciousness-raising groups, political demonstrations, and anti-imperialist discourse. The organization also published *Triple Jeopardy,* a cutting-edge radical newspaper that illustrated the intersection

Power, Black Studies, Black Student Unions, independent schools and rites of passage, and Black liberation theology and ethics. More recently, it has played a key role in the movements of Afrocentricity, ancient Egyptian studies, Black united fronts, Maatian and Ifa ethics, reparations, and the Million Person Marches. In fact, I wrote the mission statement for the Million Man March/Day of Absence on behalf of the executive committee.

Internationally, Us has maintained relations with continental and other diasporic organizations and activists, and participated in major African projects such as the second Pan-African Festival of Arts and Culture (FESTAC '77) and initiatives by the African Union. Us continues to maintain relations and work with other Third World activists and organizations. As I have noted elsewhere, in the 1960s we had stood up, seeing ourselves as descendants of Malcolm with an awesome obligation to wage the revolution he had conceived and called for. Thus, as Simba Wachanga, the Young Lions, we youthfully and self-confidently declared for ourselves and our generation that "We are the last revolutionaries in America. If we fail to leave a legacy of revolution for our children, we have failed our mission and should be dismissed as unimportant."

The message retains its original meaning and urgency even today and we remain ever grounded in our culture and steadfast in our struggle to create a just, good, and sustainable world and help rebuild the liberation movement to achieve this. For we embrace the ancient African ethical imperative: to know our past and honor it; to engage our future and improve it; and to imagine a whole new future and forge it in the most ethical, effective, and expansive ways.

> **WE ARE THE LAST REVOLUTIONARIES IN AMERICA. IF WE FAIL TO LEAVE A LEGACY OF REVOLUTION FOR OUR CHILDREN, WE HAVE FAILED OUR MISSION AND SHOULD BE DISMISSED AS UNIMPORTANT.**

of race, class, and gender on social movements long before such an intellectual intervention became the topic of conversation among professional scholars.

Black Power transformed American democracy. At the local level, in cities such as New York, Baltimore, New Orleans, Philadelphia, St. Louis, Oakland, and Los Angeles, urban militants used the movement's ethos of self-determination and cultural pride to advocate for burning issues such as decent housing, better public schools, employment, welfare benefits, and an end to police brutality. In Detroit, black trade unionists and labor activists such as Luke Tripp and General Baker, who had been mentored by

James and Grace Lee Boggs and had been a part of the early Black Power group UHURU, were part of the Dodge Revolution Union Movement (DRUM). Beginning in 1967, DRUM challenged white supremacy in the United Auto Workers labor union through a series of highly effective and nationally disruptive strikes. The revolutionary union movement consolidated its forces in the League of Revolutionary Black Workers (LRBW) and during the late 1960s briefly galvanized Black Power–era Marxist labor organizing. The idea that black liberation would be rooted in understanding, challenging, and transforming economic inequality helped to inspire the Student Organization of Black

distorted the shape and character of American democracy. Carmichael's call for Black Power included eloquent and angry denunciations against the Vietnam War that made him the subject of a wide-ranging, meticulous, and illegal surveillance by the FBI, White House, CIA, and State Department.

Carmichael may have become the most visible face of black militancy in the late 1960s, but Black Arts icons such as Sonia Sanchez, Amiri Baraka, and Larry Neal advocated a cultural revolution that carried with it profound political implications. Black Arts activists promoted a redefinition of black identity that wedded indigenous African American cultural traditions to a reconstructed vision of Africa, the Caribbean, and the wider global black diaspora.

Poet Amiri Baraka's political influence reached new heights with the organization of the Congress of African People (CAP) in 1970. CAP formed one of the leading groups in what historian Komozi Woodard has characterized as a "Modern Black Convention Movement," one that echoed nineteenth-century organizational efforts to achieve black citizenship. The modern version of this movement included the African Liberation Support Committee (ALSC), which promoted African Liberation Day (ALD) as a global event designed to promote anticolonialism, resist economic inequality globally and domestically, and educate a new generation of black activists about the history of pan-Africanism and imperialism. In fact, the ALSC and CAP went on to become United Nations NGOs.

Unity (SOBU) to drop its back-to-Africa program and to publish *African World,* one of the most sophisticated Black Power–era publications. *African World* argued that the Black Liberation Movement required a practical and theoretical understanding of the workings of global capitalism. SOBU, which later became the Youth Organization of Black Unity (YOBU), defined racism as the institutional arm of a dying empire. The organization exposed and analyzed the racial face of capitalism, highlighting the economic exploitation of African workers abroad and black workers in the United States.

Nationally, activists such as Stokely Carmichael argued that institutional racism had

Eldridge Cleaver, minister of information of the BPP, and Kathleen Cleaver, communications secretary. In 1968 Eldridge ran for president on the Peace and Freedom Party ticket and Kathleen as a candidate for California's 18th State Assembly District. They both lived in exile in Algeria where they formed the International Branch of the Black Panther Party. © Jeffrey Blankfort.

"THE BLACK POWER MOVEMENT REPRESENTS NOTHING LESS THAN AN EPIC IN AMERICAN AND WORLD HISTORY, ENCOURAGING HUMAN RIGHTS STRUGGLES FROM LONDON TO PARIS, FROM JAMAICA TO INDIA, AND FROM ISRAEL TO AUSTRALIA. "

Internationally, activists visited Africa, formed lobbying groups, and made decolonization the hallmark of efforts to transform American foreign policy toward the Third World. By 1972 the movement was driven as much by international political considerations as local and domestic ones. A remarkable but ultimately short-lived alliance between urban militants and black elected officials resulted in arguably the most diverse array of voices in African American political history speaking at the 1972 National Black Political Convention in Gary, Indiana. Simultaneously, Kwame Ture's All African People's Revolutionary Party (AAPR-P) argued that black liberation in America was rooted in the liberation of Africa under scientific socialism. The AAPR-P defined itself as a cadre-, rather than mass-, based organization. African socialism rooted in the thought of pan-African giant Kwame Nkrumah and personified by the political practice of Guinean president Sékou Touré became the hallmark of the group's efforts to build cadres in the United States and around the world. Ture, who moved to Guinea in 1969, returned to the States for frequent and well-publicized tours extolling the virtues of intense historical study, the need for political organizing, and the inevitability of a Third World revolution capable of defeating Western capitalism and imperialism against mighty odds.

Black Power's reach extended to white activists in the New Left as well as a broad range of racial and ethnic minorities ranging from Puerto Rican militants in Chicago to Mexican Americans in Los Angeles to Asian Americans in the Bay Area and Native Americans in the Midwest. The Young Lords Organization (YLO), which formed political beachheads in Chicago and New York, transformed Puerto Rican and Dominican former gang members into political activists who fought urban renewal, demanded clean streets and safe neighborhoods at the local level, exposed police brutality, and (inspired by the Black Panthers) called for an anti-imperialist world revolution. At the local level the Young Lords fought for better social services, Nuyorican architecture, antipoverty programs, and tenants' rights in New York City. The Young Lords, like the West Coast–based Brown Berets, the American Indian Movement (AIM), and Asian American radicals of the Red Guard, reflected Black Power's racial and ethnic diversity, what historian Jeffery Ogbar has characterized as the era's "rainbow radicalism."

TOP: The BPP took the brunt of the repression against Black Power militants. Oakland, September 10, 1968. Bob Fitch Photography Archive, © Stanford University Libraries, Department of Special Collections. BOTTOM: Food distribution at a Black Panther rally, Oakland, 1968. Bob Fitch Photography Archive, © Stanford University Libraries, Department of Special Collections.

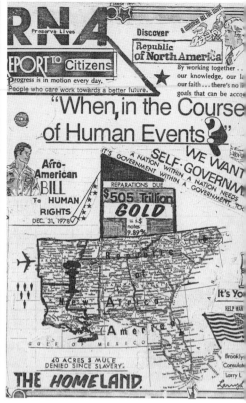

LEFT: Republic of New Afrika leaders. Sitting from left: Mabel Robinson Williams; Robert Williams Sr., RNA president; co-founder Gaidi Abiodun Obadele (Milton Henry). Standing first row: Audley "Queen Mother" Moore and co-founder Imari Abukari Obadele (Richard B. Henry). Detroit News Collection/ Walter P. Reuther, Archives of Labor and Urban Affairs, Wayne State University. MIDDLE: The RNA declared Louisiana, Mississippi, Alabama, Georgia, and South Carolina its national territory, and asked for reparations to establish an African American nation in the Deep South. Manuscripts Archives and Rare Books Division, Schomburg Center for Research in Black Culture, The New York Public Library. RIGHT: Black Panther Party and Republic of New Afrika (RNA) signs, fliers, posters and graffiti. Roxbury, Boston. 1971 © Stephen Shames.

The Black Power movement represents nothing less than an epic in American and world history, encouraging human rights struggles from London to Paris, from Jamaica to India, and from Israel to Australia. Like any watershed historical period, the era is filled with iconic individuals and organizations as well as more obscure and relatively anonymous, but no less important, activists and groups. New scholarship attempting to chronicle this era can only do justice to its vast panorama by studying both the iconic and the obscure. On this score, important historical figures such as Stokely Carmichael, Kathleen Cleaver, Huey P. Newton, and Angela Davis helped to shape the movement through participation in local, national, and global liberation struggles. Similarly, the intellectual and political work of Black Arts icons such as Sonia Sanchez, Amiri Baraka, and Haki Madhubuti transformed the era's cultural and intellectual landscape in profoundly important and historically resonant ways. The movement's intellectual legacy is comprised of the publication of thousands of books, pamphlets, speeches, essays, and poetry; and institutionalized through bookstores, independent schools, black studies programs and departments, and educational and community activism that flourish in hundreds of grassroots organizations around the country. Most importantly, thousands of grassroots activists—ranging from welfare mothers to trade unionists to school teachers—adopted

the rhetoric of Black Power militancy in an effort to transform the local conditions of everyday black people, especially during the height of Great Society reform. Thus Black Power, while usually associated with the fiery revolutionary polemics of groups such as the Black Panthers, had a compassionate side that surfaced in the political programs of local activists across the United States.

The Black Power movement transformed the political, cultural, and historical landscape of postwar America and the larger world. The movement's multifaceted organizations, from SNCC to the National Welfare Rights Organization, radically altered America's social, political, and cultural landscape. In doing so they helped give birth to and sustain one of the twentieth century's most important, and controversial, movements for social justice. Black Power's impact was panoramic, triggering revolutions in knowledge, politics, consciousness, art, public policy, and foreign affairs along lines of race, class, gender, and sexuality. The movement's heyday forced a reexamination of race, war, human rights, and democracy

and inspired millions of global citizens to reimagine a world free of poverty, racism, sexism, and economic exploitation. From Harlem to Haiti, New Orleans to Nigeria, and Birmingham to Bandung, black liberation activists called for a new and more humane political order, one that would be democratically controlled. Ultimately, Black Power's legacy reverberates through organizations that gave the era its full breadth and depth of expression and the people who animated their dreams of a liberated future in movements that simultaneously burst forth in violent staccato, threatening upheavals in their wake and unfolding with the gentle fury of a soul- and blues-tinged gospel song. Black Power was and is jazz, blues, gospel, and hip-hop. It transcended the boundaries and limits of blackness even as it filled in the unseen contours of a blues people whose country, Amiri Baraka reminds us, always was and always will be black.

Members of the Young Lords Party march from the Bronx to downtown Manhattan to show support for the Panther 21. On May 13, 1971, after forty-five minutes of jury deliberation, all defendants were acquitted. © Hiram Maristany.

CHAPTER 2

The Black Power Movement, the Black Panther Party, and Racial Coalitions

Jakobi Williams

The Black Power movement had a radical impact on grassroots organizing in poor communities of color and many white progressive circles from 1965 to about 1980. Arguably, no other group had more influence on Latinos, Asians, Native Americans, and progressive white ethnics during this period than the Black Panther Party (BPP). Founded in Oakland, California, in 1966 as the Black Panther Party for Self-Defense by two students at Merritt College—Huey Newton and Bobby Seale—the armed revolutionary and socialist organization grew to approximately forty-nine chapters across the United States at its height. Grounded in the Party's core was its leadership in the international revolutionary proletariat struggle, a deep affinity for forming coalitions and alliances that transcended race and class, and a commitment to community service programs (survival pending revolution) as a fundamental element of human rights.

THE WEST COAST

In California, one of the first groups to form an alliance and emulate the BPP was the Chicano Brown Berets. Highly influenced by

the activism of African Americans, especially around questions of identity, Mexican American youth sought to connect their plight to a larger struggle against oppression. African Americans identified as black instead of Negro, displaying a new consciousness and pride. Similarly, Mexican Americans now identified themselves as Chicano—a pre-European-contact identity grounded in racial pride that undermined the white supremacist racial hierarchy. Cesar Chavez and the labor organization the United Farm Workers (UFW) had sparked the Chicano civil rights movement, and the BPP was one of the UFW's allies despite the two groups' differences about revolutionary ideology. In this spirit, David Sanchez—an East Los Angeles high school student—formed the first unit of the Brown Berets. Taking cues from the BPP's uniform (a black beret and black leather jacket), the Chicano group sported brown berets and brown jackets and organized demonstrations against the Los Angeles Unified School District and the Los Angeles Police Department. The beret also demonstrated the group's affinity for the Panthers' revolutionary platform. The Brown Berets instituted a thirteen-point platform and program, with seven points taken directly from the Panthers' own ten-point platform. Once the alliance was created with the BPP, the

Brown Berets vowed to assist the Panthers' efforts to combat racism in America. By the time the group disbanded in 1972, largely due to government repression, the Brown Berets had close to ninety chapters and about five thousand members.[1]

From its inception, the BPP did not fit the black separatist mold usually associated with Black Power groups but rather encompassed a connection to the struggle of all poor and oppressed people. Japanese American Richard Aoki became one of the first members to join the newly established Black Panther Party for Self-Defense in 1966. Aoki met Newton and Seale when he was a student at Merritt College during student activism campaigns. When he was a child, his family's property was confiscated and they were victims of internment during World War II. A U.S. Army veteran, Aoki provided the BPP with its first cache of firearms; he also played a key role in the Party's early ideological formations. In 1968, Aoki joined the Asian American Political Alliance (AAPA), which was created by various Asian ethnics at the University of California, Berkeley. While a field marshal for the Panthers, Aoki became the spokesperson for AAPA. The groups worked in coalition with the Panthers on campaigns against police brutality, the Vietnam War, exploitation of farm workers, and diversity on college campuses. Another Asian American group that worked in solidarity with the BPP was the Chinese Red Guard. Similar to the Brown Berets, the Red Guard modeled itself after the BPP. Founded in San Francisco in 1969, the Red Guard was an armed communist organization that served the Asian community with a duty that rivaled the BPP's level of commitment. Members donned army field jackets and red berets as they fought for the integrity of tuberculosis testing centers, maintained Asian legal services sites, protected Asian draft dodgers, and lobbied to

In California, one of the first groups to emulate and ally itself with the BPP was the Chicano Brown Berets. Brown Berets' founder, David Sanchez, declared that brown represented the dignity and pride in the color of his skin and race. Brown Berets at a "Free Huey" rally, Oakland, 1968. Bob Fitch Photography Archive, © Stanford University Libraries, Department of Special Collections.

get China a seat at the United Nations. At its peak the Red Guard consisted of about two hundred Chinese youths before its demise in 1971 due to government repression.[2]

In Los Angeles, Japanese American youth formed the organizations Yellow Brotherhood and Asian American Hardcore in 1969. Although both groups were modeled after the Panthers, their memberships were gang bangers, ex-convicts, and military veterans. Also, both focused primarily on drug detoxification. Government repression ensured that both organizations were short lived.[3]

There are many misconceptions about the BPP and among the most prevalent is that the organization was the black version of the Ku Klux Klan, or that the group hated white people. Propaganda disseminated by the FBI and other agencies—fueled in part by some

Fred Hampton's Rainbow Coalition encouraged African Americans, Puerto Ricans, and poor youth to bring an end to ethnic tensions and gang violence. Seated left to right: Fred Hampton; Pedro "Yoruba" Guzman, minister of information of the Young Lords Party (New York); Jose (Cha Cha) Jimenez of the Young Lords Organization Chicago); and Mike Klonsky of the Revolutionary Youth Movement of the Students for a Democratic Society. Chicago, 1969. Chicago. Photographer Howard Simmons. Courtesy of Sun-Times Media. Lisbet Tellefsen Collection.

of the Panthers' fiery rhetoric—helped to foster such misconceptions. Although the BPP did not allow whites to join the organization, the Party relied heavily upon Hollywood philanthropy and a contingent of Jewish attorneys across the country. More importantly, white organizations formed close

JOSE (CHA CHA) JIMENEZ
Unite with the Many to Defeat the Few

There were loud noises in a crowded North Cell House in Chicago's House of Correction forming the background for the soul dusties songs of an African American radio station played till midnight on the loudspeaker. It was a jailhouse branch maybe 95 percent black, .5 percent white, and the rest Latino. We were all in the "hole" (a.k.a. maximum security) being punished for breaking rules within dormitories or other cellblocks. I was accused of trying to escape but I really was innocent. In fact the jail had become second nature to me. I did not desire escape, only status, to become the most enslaved and the meanest of the bunch. Now, I was being

rewarded, isolated from the rest of the population in a cramped cage. It was gray steel, which was set atop of old chipped, Civil War–wood that you could make out only in the catwalk outside. The roaches were out of control falling all over you from the ceiling. Large cats roamed freely to kill rodents almost as tall as they were. You befriended them with leftover bread to try to remember love because everyone else was filled with displaced anger. To be kind inside a jail is like working against reason. Your best bet is acceptance of this hell so that you can find relaxation on a framed wired bed with a feathered pillow and a mattress. The toilet and sink are

your only furniture, and it is only one piece—just wide enough to fit between the wall and the bed frame and to hold your butt cheek. You dress shirtless in your underwear in the sweaty summer heat. No visits here except inmates passing through, recently arrested during rioting after Martin Luther King's murder or the yearly roundup of Mexican migrant workers. But you could yell out checkers or chess moves to other cells and read, write, and reflect.

I read for the very first time since eighth grade about a hermit priest. It was not the book that moved me so much as the fact that I once wanted to become a Catholic priest but failed. I reflected upon the old movies of Christians who were killed for their beliefs, and how a loyal apostle humbled by Christ asked to be crucified upside down. Like my mother had taught me: to be Christian meant to not only believe in something but to be

willing to die for it. And here I was in jail for an insignificant sin like drugs. Ya basta, it was finally time for me to go to confession, to cleanse my soul.

The only way to leave this cell was in chains for a weekly shower or court, or to go home. For certain I could not leave the cell but still I wanted to cleanse myself inside, and as a Catholic it meant confession. Finally it was approved and I was now willing to accept ridicule like the Christians, so that I could be whole once again. To my surprise the angry prisoners were nonjudgmental. They were kind and respectful.

I continued to ask questions to the Muslim librarian who gave me Martin Luther King's book to read. He followed that up with Malcolm X. Then there were the Black Panthers in the news on the radio. They were

carrying weapons and demanding their right to bear arms. It was then that I began to hear the chattering sounds and feel the weight of the chains. Once they were handcuffs and to myself I was a hardened criminal. But now they were chains and for the first time I was trapped and doubting the severity of my crimes. Of course it was still a sin but now I felt trapped in a vicious cycle. I now refused to be just a scapegoat and wanted change for me and for my people and not for a decadent system. It was not just me who was at fault, but a capitalist profit-making system as well.

I had witnessed large drug dealers arrested with several ounces of drugs worth thousands of dollars on the streets. They would pay an attorney to arrange a $50 bond for their release and

then "beat the case." Here I was in jail for residue in an aluminum foil bag found not on me but on the sidewalk. Since I could not afford an attorney, I was doing sixty days in the "hole." And this had been repeated throughout my life. I thought about other injustices that were all around us and the People's Movement that was saying the only way to get rid of our conditions was to make a revolution. Check out history, they would say, and you will see that the black slave uprisings in 1791 in Saint Domingue against the French are what led to the other uprisings in Brazil and the Caribbean islands. It woke people up and ended slavery. The argument, they said, was between violence and non-violence. But that was what the enemy had tricked us to think. The real argument was whether

> **" OPPRESSION IS A PROCESS LIKE URBAN RENEWAL, WHICH WAS THE PRIMARY ISSUE THAT GAVE US OUR OFFICIAL BIRTH ON PUERTO RICAN INDEPENDENCE DAY, SEPTEMBER 23, 1968. "**

alliances with the BPP. For example, Panthers on the West Coast worked with the Peace and Freedom Party—a white radical political organization opposed to the two-party system. In 1968, Panthers helped the Peace and Freedom Party collect signatures to be placed on that year's election ballot. Later, Black Panther Party members ran for political office on Peace and Freedom Party tickets: In 1968, Eldridge Cleaver ran for U.S. president; in 1973, Bobby Seale was a candidate for mayor of Oakland; and Elaine Brown ran for a city council seat in Oakland that same year.

Students for a Democratic Society (SDS), the largest national leftist student organization of the period, also had a short-lived relationship with the BPP. Founded in 1960 and primarily located on college campuses, the group was inspired by the civil rights

we should be free or slaves. I was reading and reading and the Black Panthers were showing me that I needed to educate and organize the people and the people will do whatever it takes to free themselves.

All I had was the Young Lords, but I was as ashamed of them as I was ashamed of myself because they were a gang and of course without a purpose. At first I tried to reinvent the wheel and started a group called the Puerto Rican Progressive Movement because we wanted self-determination and to free Puerto Rico from being a colony of the U.S. Only about four or five members joined and most were Young Lords anyway.

It was then that I realized that we did not need to destroy the Young Lords and change the name of the group; we needed to destroy the old negative purpose and enhance what gave us pride—our community and our name. There was no shame in our name, only shame in our purpose.

Our mission became simply to free Puerto Rico and to empower our people. That meant that we needed a party, but we had to unite with the many, and those who would be easiest to organize would be the most oppressed by the system. Exactly. They were the folks who grew up with us.

This system of oppression against our peoples was created like slavery and it is why I could relate to Malcolm X when he spoke about a house Negro and a field Negro. We also had our alcaguetes who continue to perpetuate colonialism. They are the ones who fear losing their food stamps and social security checks and want to remain dependent on the United States when we paid into these systems with our own sweat and blood. Puerto Ricans were handed citizenship in the beginning of World War I to fight for the United States, and we have been fighting for them ever since. They did not give to us; we gave them our blood. We also gave them cheap labor.

Oppression is a process like urban renewal, which was the primary issue that gave us our official birth on Puerto Rican Independence Day, September 23, 1968. That urban renewal was marketed in our Lincoln Park neighborhood of Chicago as creating an inner city suburb: fifteen minutes from the downtown Loop, next to the zoo and next to Lake Michigan. Sounds wonderful, but Lincoln Park was where blacks and Latinos lived, and the new inner-city suburb today is nearly all white. In fact, they have repeated this in many cities of the U.S. and the world.

Was not slavery marketed in the same way, though on a much more vicious scale? It was worldwide, with European nations like Portugal, Great Britain, France, Spain, and Holland participating. This included many countries in Africa. It also included the colonies in the Americas, especially the thirteen original colonies, Brazil, and the Caribbean islands. Slavery wasn't movement and advocated for equality, economic justice, and participatory democracy for all citizens. SDS's membership drastically increased alongside the escalation of the Vietnam War, and its protests were aggressive and sometimes violent. On the West Coast, SDS assisted the BPP by helping to form defense committees for incarcerated Panthers and disseminated information about critical issues that plagued black communities. The groups differed on the use of violence, which strained their relationship. The Weathermen faction of SDS wanted to use violence to forge a revolution to overthrow the American establishment. The Panthers advocated self-determination by all poor people, forging racial alliances along class lines, and using armed resistance—not violence—as a tool of self-defense. The Weathermen's involvement in a series of bombings caused the Party to distance itself from the group and SDS, as the Panthers vehemently opposed violence as an instrument of change.

THE MIDWEST AND SOUTH

By 1968, BPP chapters had spread east across the country to almost every major city. The largest and most strategically engaged chapter outside of Oakland was the Illinois chapter of the Black Panther Party (ILBPP) which officially began in August 1968. Just as the national headquarters in Oakland had set up numerous chapters throughout the state of California, the ILBPP, with its headquarters in Chicago, established several chapters in Illinois and also coordinated efforts for most chapters in the region. For this reason the

about creating an inner-city suburb but about gold and spices and tropical products: coffee, tobacco, cocoa, sugar, and cotton.

Slavery was about luxury and profit and cheap labor. They first brought in prisoners but not enough. The conditions killed off many of the indigenous peoples and so you had the Catholic friar, Bartolome de las Casas, and others in suits and ties deploring the destruction of the natives but saying nothing of the African slaves. It took centuries to change the mindset and legally abolish slavery, but it still exists in different forms. It will take a long time for Puerto Ricans to reject being colonized.

But from early on I discovered what our little Red Book taught us: that the way to win is to seek out allies and to "Unite with the many to defeat the few." It is why we followed Chairman Fred Hampton's lead and formed the Rainbow Coalition.

Rainbow Coalition press conference for interracial unity on the anniversary of Dr. Martin Luther King Jr.'s death. Seated from left: Jack "Junebug" Boykin (Jobs Or Income Now [JOIN], Goodfellows, Young Patriots, Rising Up Angry), Henry Gaddis, a.k.a. Poison of the BPP, and Luis of the Young Lords Organization. Standing from left: Andy Kenniston (JOIN, Patriots), Hy Thurman (JOIN, Goodfellows, Patriots), Michael James (JOIN, RUA), Bud Paulin (JOIN, RUA), Bobby Rush (BPP), and Alfredo (YLO). Chicago, April 4, 1969. Photograph by Linn Ehrlich /Michael James Collection.

The Blackstone Rangers were a Chicago gang. In the 1960s it renamed itself the Blackstone Nation and was involved in fighting for housing, education, jobs, and justice and was briefly allied to the Illinois chapter of the Black Panther Party. Blackstone Rangers unity graffiti in Chicago. © Darryl Cowherd.

ILBPP chapter can be referred to as "national headquarters east." Illinois Panthers also continued the BPP's policy of organizing race and class coalitions and alliances.

The ILBPP established the original Rainbow Coalition in 1968. It was Deputy Chairman Fred Hampton who coined the term "Rainbow Coalition." In Chicago, the name became the code word for class struggle and class solidarity. Fred Hampton was the face of the Rainbow Coalition, and Robert E. Lee III—known as Bob Lee—served as the legman of the organization. Hampton gave speeches and sat for interviews on behalf of the Rainbow Coalition, but it was Bob Lee who was the mover and shaker of the group.[4] Lee was out in the street politicizing groups from Chicago's north side and introducing them to the Black Panther Party. Bob Lee had moved from Houston, Texas, to Chicago in 1968 as a VISTA (Volunteers in Service to America) volunteer, and he worked exclusively with youth in the area, which consisted of African Americans, Puerto Ricans, and southern whites.[5]

The original Rainbow Coalition initially consisted of the ILBPP; the Young Patriots Organization (YPO), a group of southern white migrants mostly from various parts of Appalachia; and the Young Lords Organization (YLO), a socially conscious Puerto Rican group. Later, Rising Up Angry (RUA), a club of young white progressives, formed an alliance with the organization. All of the groups were formed in 1968. Even though the Illinois Panthers led the Rainbow Coalition, there was no official head of the group. The organization was structured as a partnership in a united front. Nevertheless, Deputy Chairman Fred

In Minneapolis, a group of Native Americans founded the American Indian Movement in 1968 and modeled it after the BPP's community self-defense model. They called for Red Power. AIM and the BPP supported each other's cause. Kathleen Cleaver and AIM activists at a rally to fight the extradition of AIM co-founder Dennis Bank from California to South Dakota, where he faced charges of incitement to riot. 1976. © Ilka Hartmann 2016.

Hampton was understood to be the de facto leader and spokesperson for the alliance. The Young Patriots, Young Lords, and Rising Up Angry accepted the leadership of the Panthers; however, the groups were clear that their role was not to organize in the black community but in their own, to draw attention to the contradictions there, and to educate their own people. This focus made the Rainbow Coalition very effective. The three groups also mirrored the community service programs that the Black Panther Party had established. They also established newspapers that paralleled the BPP's *Black Panther.*

YPO was located in Uptown on Chicago's north side. Most of Uptown's residents were southern white migrants and the neighborhood was home to some of the worst slums in the city with severe abject white poverty.

Bob Lee spent weeks in Uptown organizing community service programs on behalf of its residents and incorporating the YPO into the original Rainbow Coalition. Led by Hy Thurman and others, the group initially comprised white working-class males and used as its symbol the Confederate flag. The YPO's introduction by the Panthers to class solidarity that transcended racial divisions forced the group to reassess its traditional identification with the Confederate flag. Shortly after being politicized by the Panthers, the YPO incorporated other ethnicities and races into its ranks. Besides white ethnic southerners, there were Spanish, Indian, Italian, Cuban, and some African American members. The diversity of the group's ranks reflected the symbolism of the Rainbow Coalition. Like the ILBPP, the YPO opened

MICHAEL JAMES

Rising Up Angry and Chicago's Early Rainbow Coalition, 1968–1975: Remembering the Black Panther Party, Young Lords Organization, Young Patriots, and Rising Up Angry

In the 1960s I was drawn to Chicago's history of struggle and its tradition of community organizing. It was an exciting time and I became part of the Movement. People of all races, ethnic backgrounds, and religions acted on their belief in a Rainbow Coalition to make "Power to the People" a reality.

1968 was a hell of a year.

That was when the struggles of the 1960s culminated symbolically in Chicago. The groundwork, however, had been laid not only by the civil rights movement, but by a variety of converging forces: the rising expectations of soldiers who came back from World War II; the demonstrations against atomic bomb testing in Washington, DC, in the fall of 1961; the emergence and growth of the women's movement; the Cuban Revolution; the war on poverty; the Free Speech Movement at Berkeley and progressive actions on campuses everywhere; and the growing awareness of the crisis of poverty in America—thanks in part to Michael Harrington's *The Other America*, which helped initiate the government's war on poverty.

In 1968 in Chicago the Black Panther Party of Illinois and the Young Lords Organization emerged, and gave leadership to the direction of organizing for years to come.

free breakfast-for-children programs and free community clinics that were well received by Uptown residents. Drawing strength from community support, the Young Patriots allied with the Black Panther Party to organize as one solidified group against the policies of Chicago's Mayor Richard J. Daley. YPO also modeled their newspaper *The Patriot* after the *Black Panther*. More importantly, the YPO served as an example to other groups of how Illinois Panthers helped people end the paralysis that racism imposed upon them.

Originally located in Lincoln Park on Chicago's north side, the Young Lords Organization began as a group fighting to end urban renewal polices that displaced and relocated large numbers of the Puerto Rican residents out of the community. YLO president Jose (Cha Cha) Jimenez's

The second Black Power Conference was a mass summit meeting—one thousand delegates represented over two hundred eighty organizations and institutions from twenty-six states, Bermuda, and Nigeria—was held July 20–23, 1967, in Newark, just three days after the uprising in that city had left twenty-six dead and over one thousand injured. Seated left to right: comedian Dick Gregory (second from left); Maulana Karenga, founder of Us; H. Rap Brown, of SNCC, and Ralph Featherstone of SNCC. July 21, 1967, Newark, NJ. © Bettmann/Corbis.

———

charismatic leadership paralleled that of ILBPP deputy chairman Fred Hampton. After the YLO joined the Rainbow Coalition the composition of the group's membership also changed. YLO expanded from an exclusive Puerto Rican group to include African

A few years earlier in Chicago's Uptown, JOIN (Jobs or Income Now) Community Union was founded. It was a people's organization initiated by Students for a Democratic Society (SDS) as part of their inspirational vision to create an interracial movement of the poor.

JOIN organized rent strikes, a welfare union, a food co-op, and a community theater. It fostered the Goodfellows, a loose organization of young men with a developing political consciousness who marched on the old Summerdale police station to protest blatant police brutality in Uptown.

That fall of 1968 Peggy Terry, a southern white welfare mother who lived in Uptown and was a JOIN leader, became the vice presidential candidate on the Peace and Freedom Party ticket headed by Black Panther Eldridge Cleaver. The following year some members of JOIN and Goodfellows coalesced to form the short-lived Young Patriots

Organization. This is when some of us started a newspaper to promote the revolution and help build a progressive organization of poor and working-class whites beyond Uptown.

The paper and subsequent organization were called *Rising Up Angry*. We were inspired by the primarily Puerto Rican Young Lords Organization in Lincoln Park, who used the slogan "Educate to Liberate," and by Lenin, who talked about the importance of a newspaper "in a pre-party situation." The Black Panther Party, which valiantly stood up to oppression and initiated "serve the people" programs, also inspired us.

It was Illinois Black Panther Party deputy chairman Fred Hampton and Panther field organizers Bobby Lee and Henry Gaddis (a.k.a. Poison) who conceived of the original Rainbow Coalition. They connected with the organizing that was going on in Uptown. (Not long after, Ed Harahan and

the Chicago Police, with the cooperation of the FBI and the government's infamous COINTELPRO assassinated Hampton).

A loose network of Panthers, Lords, Patriots, and incubating Rising Up Angry (RUA) people emerged. There was contact with other organizations and street gangs, including the Native Americans who became Chicago's American Indian Movement (AIM). On a broader level, there was interaction between organizers in many Chicago neighborhoods, black, brown, and white, all working to disrupt and transform old man Daley's regime.

When Rev. Martin Luther King Jr. was killed, this early iteration of the Rainbow Coalition held a press conference at Chicago public television's WTTW Studios on St. Louis. A photo by Linn H. Ehrlich captured the spirit of the times and the interracial, multiethnic face of organizing in Chicago's neighborhoods.

I believed white radicals and

activists of conscience needed to work with white youth in poor and working-class neighborhoods to help overcome deep-seated racism in those communities. We wanted to have them join the Movement, to struggle along with blacks and Latinos to overthrow the racist, capitalist imperialists who were running the show. I believed there was real potential to bring white youth into the Movement, and that the successes we had had with poor southern whites in JOIN and Uptown could be re-created in other primarily white communities and neighborhoods throughout Chicago. I believed it when we said, "Power to the People."

So in the early spring of 1969 a group of us met in a farmhouse in Fairborn, Ohio.

We went to see *Wild in the Streets,* basically a reactionary film made by the same people who produced the TV series *FBI*. The movie focused on youth rebellion and featured a theme song with the line, "There's a new sun, rising up angry in the sky."

"Rising up angry!" The phrase stuck and became the name of our paper, the mission of which was to "educate in order to liberate." The cover of Issue No.1 was a photo of a young woman named Judy holding an M16 rifle and sitting behind her boyfriend Pete on the back of my Triumph TR6 motorcycle. It came out on July 29, 1969, and featured a "get off the fence" call to action, with articles on the Young Lords, the Black Panthers, women's rights, hot-rod cars, guns, police brutality, and the Vietnam War. Gears, guns, grease, and revolution were the themes, meant to appeal to Chicago's "greasers," the city's white, working-class youth.

We moved that paper all over town—and beyond. We wrote on walls, "the pages in the people's book." Power to the people! Free Huey! Off the pigs! U.S. out of 'Nam! Respect our Sisters! Rising Up Angry!

In a relatively short time we began to influence people and change the way local white youth looked at race, gender, war, and justice issues. We were definitely on Chicago's radar and making our mark. We had internal political education meetings on a regular basis and met to consider and make plans for actions. Following the lead of the Black Panther Party, we developed a series of Serve the People programs.

A Breakfast for Children's program was started in the Church of the Holy Covenant at Wilton and Diversey. In that same church there was the Fritzi Englestein Free People's Health Clinic. RUA people were deeply involved, interviewing and testing patients from the community, acting as advocates in the city's bureaucratic medical system. We promoted the concept of preventive medicine, which included not only early screening and preemptive treatment, but also reflected our early interest in wholesome food

> **" IN ITS EFFORTS TO STRENGTHEN THE CITY'S POOR COMMUNITIES, WHICH WERE VULNERABLE TO POLITICAL EXPLOITATION, THE RAINBOW COALITION ENVISIONED GIVING NONTRADITIONAL GROUPS LIKE GANGS GREATER CLOUT IN CHICAGO'S POLITICAL ARENA. "**

Americans, whites, and other Latinos. At least one-fifth of the organization was Mexican American or Chicano, as the YLO saw a need to work together with other Latinos to build a unified political base for the Latin community. The YLO adopted Panther ideology and methodology. For instance, to join the group a potential member was required to participate in political education classes, karate instruction, and community service work. The organization offered a free breakfast-for-children program, set up a Puerto Rican cultural center, and opened a medical center in Lincoln Park. Also, the YLO created the first community daycare center in the city. The group's newspaper was entitled *YLO*. After Panther Fred Hampton's assassination by the FBI and Chicago police, Jose (Cha Cha) Jimenez picked up

and our celebration of sport as a healthy community activity. RUA created a Peoples' Sport Institute with a running club, Easy Striders.

Rising Up Angry's Peoples' Legal Program engaged lawyers and developed community representatives who met with people in need of legal help—giving them advice, getting them lawyers, handling their cases, and advocating for them in court. Inspired by a Black Panther program, we started a bus-to-prison program to help people visit their loved ones in various state prisons. This was a well-intentioned concept that turned out to be short lived; we quickly learned the rate of white incarceration was miniscule to that of blacks and Latinos.

Friends of Angry was an RUA outreach program that brought kids from all over Chicago together at Peoples' Dances and antiwar demonstrations, as well as to meetings on the war, the Black Panther Party, and educational sessions on what your

rights were if you were busted. We hosted film events, screening movies like the labor classic *Salt of the Earth* and the revolutionary thriller *Battle of Algiers*.

RUA's GI Program involved veterans returning from Vietnam, and helped focus actions against that war. A core group emerged from returning vets, including a network of Marines who were incarcerated at the Glenview Naval Training Center. Eventually we organized a massive march and demonstration against the war in Foss Park in North Chicago, next to the sprawling Great Lakes Naval Training Center. Our slogan was "SOS—Stop Our Ships, Save Our Sailors."

The United Farm Workers (UFW) of Cesar Chavez was an inspirational organization in those years, and Rising Up Angry joined with others citywide in mounting an ongoing boycott of Jewel Supermarkets for their refusal to honor the UFW. When the farmworkers came to town we held a welcoming rally.

The multitude of political and social justice events of 1968, and organizing by groups both in and beyond the Rainbow Coalition, helped create a movement in Chicago that ultimately forged a generation of activists whose actions, beliefs, spirit, and involvement in movement politics and government continues today. There is a direct line from 1968 to the election of Harold Washington, the Obama campaign, and the 2015 Jesus "Chuy" Garcia campaign for mayor.

More than ever, We the People are in a position to create a politics of affirmation, unity, and inclusion, with a guiding vision of justice, fairness, and peace. The Rainbow Coalition, many members of which are now Elders, continues to organize and to be a significant part of bringing people everywhere to that place where we Share One Heart.

All Power to the People!

the mantle and kept the original Rainbow Coalition alive.

The third group that the ILBPP worked with was called *Rising Up Angry*, a group of white progressives located in the Logan Square community on Chicago's north side. Most RUA members were students immersed in the countercultural trends of the time and were inspired by the original Rainbow Coalition started by the ILBPP. Led by Mike James and others, they were also peace advocates who rejected the Vietnam War and opposed the repressive policies of the Daley administration. Their newspaper, *Rising Up Angry*, issued news that covered the struggles of all the aforementioned groups as well as critical issues that affected all communities regardless of race or class. It was equally as informative as the *Black Panther.* One of RUA's major goals was to incorporate fellow white ethnics into the movement led by the Panthers; the organization spent a significant amount of time in north side high schools attempting to politicize white youth. Like the YPO and YLO before them, RUA adopted the Panthers' community service programs but also launched other programs to benefit their community. The organization sought to take a broader approach to its programs and encompass more areas than those offered by the Panthers' community service models. For example, as part of the group's antiwar policy, RUA created a GI program to assist returning soldiers with anger management and the transition to civilian life. Returning vets and a network of Marines formerly incarcerated at the Glenview Naval Air Station made up the core of the GI program. Other programs addressed draft and abortion counseling, sex education, interracial labor organizing, and drug education.

In its efforts to strengthen the city's poor communities, which were vulnerable to political exploitation, the Rainbow Coalition envisioned giving nontraditional groups like gangs greater clout in Chicago's political arena. The Young Patriots, Young Lords, and Rising Up Angry all spent significant time attempting to transform gangs in their communities into political entities. The Illinois Panthers influenced the groups to do so, as the Party had made strides in transforming gangs in African American

National Black Power conferences, held annually from 1966 to 1974, gathered various organizations. With four thousand delegates, the conference in Philadelphia was the largest. It aimed to develop a "national black political party to lead black communities in the struggle to control their own space." Black Power: National Black Conference, Philadelphia, 1968. Jean Blackwell Hutson Research and Reference Division, Schomburg Center for Research in Black Culture, The New York Public Library.

In New York, the BPP, the Young Lords, the Young Patriots, I Wor Kuen (a Marxist Asian American group founded in New York in 1969 and modeled after the BPP), and the Inmates Liberation Front united to demand the release of the Panther 21, members of the BPP arrested in April 1969 on suspicion of planning to bomb several sites in the city. Manuscripts Archives and Rare Books Division, Schomburg Center for Research in Black Culture, The New York Public Library.

communities on both the west and south sides of Chicago.

The Illinois Panthers' influence also had an effect on the white student leftist group Students for a Democratic Society, which supported the Rainbow Coalition. Despite popular perceptions, SDS had no formal coalition or alliance with the Panthers in Chicago, due to the two groups' methodological differences over using violence as a method of agitation. In 1968, SDS's national meeting was held at the old Chicago Coliseum. At this meeting, ideological constraints caused SDS to fracture into two competing groups: the Progressive Labor Party and the Weathermen. Primarily on account of the friction within the student group, SDS never became a direct divisional entity of the Rainbow Coalition. Nevertheless, Panthers and SDS members participated alongside one another in common causes. Clearly, SDS and the Illinois Panthers took a common stance against oppression and the Vietnam War. They disagreed intensely, however, about the uses of violence and thus SDS was not invited to join the Rainbow Coalition. The Rainbow Coalition and its components were initially just a local phenomenon, and the group was able to establish alliances between white ethnics, Puerto Ricans, and the city's various racial and ethnic street gangs. There were also efforts to develop partnerships in Chinatown, and the coalition worked with individual Asians in Uptown. It did not, however, partner with any local Asian organizations, as BPP chapters in other parts of the United States were able to do successfully.

The national leadership of the Black Panther Party in Oakland, California, had established coalition building as a major principle of the organization. Thus, the Rainbow Coalition's success in Chicago exemplified the Party's aspirations. Bob Lee's innate ability as an organizer garnered national attention, and so the national leadership—the central committee of the Black Panther Party in Oakland, in collaboration with the Illinois chapter's central staff—decided to put Bob Lee and Bill "Preacherman" Fesperman, of the YPO, on the road together to replicate the Rainbow Coalition model. By early 1970, the two activists had traveled to other cities to organize parallel racial coalitions.

Thanks to Bob Lee's efforts, the Rainbow Coalition concept also took root in Texas. In Houston, the Black Panther Party was originally called the People's Party II and led by Carl Hampton, who was shot and killed by police snipers in 1970. Bob Lee returned home to Houston, Texas, and helped the People's Party II to form alliances with a white radical group called the John Brown Revolutionary League led by Bartee Hale, a former SDS member at Southern Methodist University. Together, the groups worked with a Chicano nationalist group, the Mexican American Youth Organization (MAYO), which was founded in 1967 by five Mexican American student activists affiliated with St. Mary's University in San Antonio, Texas. MAYO grew to more than fifty chapters in southwest Texas, including a chapter in Houston. The coalition also included the Chicano organization Casa de los Siete in Dallas and an untitled group of poor white ethnics in rural southwest Texas. Both groups respected the work of Carl Hampton and the Party because they identified with the ideology of class struggle against economic oppression and disenfranchisement. The Red Panthers cadre, an antiracist and anti-imperialist women's liberation organization based in New Orleans, also formed an alliance with the Houston Rainbow Coalition.[6]

In Minneapolis, a cadre of Native Americans founded the American Indian Movement (AIM) in 1968 modeled after the BPP's community self-defense concept. For example, one of AIM's first initiatives was a police patrol to curb police brutality. AIM also instituted a twenty-point platform that far exceeded the demands outlined in the BPP's ten-point platform. Their call for "Red Power" resonated with the BPP such that the groups made concerted efforts to support each other's cause. By 1970, AIM was a national organization and thus experienced the same degree of government repression that plagued the Panthers. The most infamous event took place during a firefight between five AIM members and two FBI agents at Wounded Knee, South Dakota, resulting in several injuries and the incarceration of key AIM leadership. Despite such repression, the coalition persevered and, unlike the BPP, AIM survived beyond the 1980s. The spirit that

Under the new banner of antifascism, an extremely broad coalition of progressive groups united and organized in many cities. David Hilliard, chief of staff of the BPP, called for the Revolutionary People's Constitutional Convention in Washington, DC. The successful convention was held later that year in Philadelphia, June 1970. AP Photo.

——

motivated the establishment of the Rainbow Coalitions was one that invited people of all backgrounds—of different races, classes, ages, and geographic locations—to fight injustice and economic inequality.[7]

THE EAST COAST

In New York, the BPP established links with the I Wor Kuen (IWK) and the Young Lords Party (YLP). Founded in 1969, IWK was a Chinese organization whose name meant "the harmonious and righteous fist" and referred to the Chinese Boxer Rebellion. The group was directly modeled after the Red Guard in California and most of their members were college-educated middle-class leftists, but unlike the Red Guard the IWK was a female-dominated group. Like the BPP, one goal of the IWK was to mobilize its community for a class-based revolution against racial and class oppression. Unfortunately, IWK's revolutionary spirit caused dissension in Asian American communities as many rejected the group's Communist platform and feared that it would spark a backlash against such communities. As a result, the IWK was never able to establish a formidable presence in the Asian American community and by 1975, in order to maintain its relevance, the organization was forced to merge

> ## " THE BLACK PANTHER PARTY OFFERED VARIED GROUPS A PERSPECTIVE THAT HELPED THEM TO DEVELOP THEIR SENSE OF IDENTITY AS GRASSROOTS POLITICAL WORK GAVE THEM A NEW SENSE OF THEMSELVES AND THE FUTURE POSSIBILITIES OF THEIR COMMUNITIES. "

with other racial leftist groups to form the League of Revolutionary Struggle (LRS). The LRS maintained an active presence in New York until its dissolution in 1990.[8]

The Young Lords Party was probably the most productive and longest-lived unit of all the Black Power movement's coalition groups. New York during this era had the largest Puerto Rican population in the United States. Inspired by the Young Lords Organization (especially their advocacy for the independence of the island of Puerto Rico from the United States) and the Rainbow Coalition in Chicago, Puerto Rican student activists formed a chapter called the Young Lords Party in New York in October 1969. Like the Panthers nationally and the Young Lords in Chicago before them, the YLP published a paper entitled *Palante,* which spread news about critical issues in their communities and the organization's campaigns, programs, and efforts to address such issues. The group used various direct action methods against New York City government that resulted in several tangible changes in sanitation, health-care facilities, elimination of lead-based paints, and reforms at the Board of Corrections. There were community service programs that mirrored both the BPP and the YLO such as free breakfast-for-children programs and daycare centers. One significant coalition campaign against city government was the YLP/BPP joint takeover of Lincoln Hospital,

which forced the city to build a new hospital in the South Bronx. Such efforts galvanized Puerto Rican residents in other cities and by August 1970 YLP offices had been opened in Philadelphia, Pennsylvania; Newark, New Jersey; and Hayward, California. These YLP chapters worked closely with the BPP and other Black Power groups in their areas.[9]

CONCLUSION

The Black Panther Party offered varied groups a perspective that helped them to develop their sense of identity as grassroots political work gave them a new sense of themselves and the future possibilities of their communities. These groups demonstrated by way of their bold confrontational methods the egregious contradictions of American democracy and a shared vision of a society that valued humanity over wealth. Such facts are highlighted by the various conventions and conferences organized during the Black Power movement, including the 1967 National Conference on Black Power in Newark, New Jersey, and the National Black Political Convention of 1972 in Gary, Indiana. Two other meetings that epitomized the race/class solidarity and revolutionary spirit of the period were the United Front Against Fascism Conference (UFAFC) of 1969 in Oakland, California, and the Revolutionary People's Constitutional Convention (RPCC) of 1970 in Philadelphia,

LEFT: *The Black Arts Movement was aesthetically and ideologically diverse, but was connected by the belief that a major part of its work was promoting revolutionary social transformation. Portrait of Amiri Baraka by Emory Douglas, 1967. © 2015 Emory Douglas/Artists Rights Society (ARS), New York.* RIGHT: *Black Power activists attempted to reconstruct the American university. They pressed, notably, for black studies. This Emory Douglas drawing was published in Black Panther on May 11, 1969. © 2015 Emory Douglas/Artists Rights Society (ARS), New York.*

Black Power spread through a series of conflicts with the criminal justice system. Many of the movement's strategists, theoreticians, and foot soldiers spent time in jail or prison. "Break the Chains" poster designed by Mary Patten and Madame Binh Graphics Collective, 1968. © Mary Patten. Art and Artifact Division, Schomburg Center for Research in Black Culture, The New York Public Library.

FREE BOBBY   FREE ERICKA
FREE RUCHELL MAGEE
FREE ANGELA
FREE KATHLEEN
AND ALL POLITICAL PRISONERS

FREEDOM

OFF THE PIGS

SHOOT TO KILL

TOP: *"Free Huey"—a diverse crowd of activists, some raising Chinese leader Chairman Mao's "Little Red Book," rally in front of the Federal Building in San Francisco in 1969. © Stephen Shames. LEFT: Emory Douglas drew this illustration in New Haven, Connecticut, where Ericka Huggins and Bobby Seale were jailed, accused of participating in the murder of a fellow Panther. The work appeared in* Black Panther *on March 6, 1971. © 2015 Emory Douglas/Artists Rights Society (ARS), New York.*

TOP: *The youngest Panther kids. Oakland, 1971.* © *Stephen Shames. BOTTOM: The cause of the Black Power-era political prisoners continues to resonate in the United States and abroad. Protest against the death sentence of Black Panther Mumia Abu-Jamal in front of the American embassy in Brasília, Brazil, 1995. AP Photo/Eraldo Peres*

TOP: Malcolm X was a central influence on the Black Power movement and beyond. His legacy lives on. Gathering outside the Audubon Ballroom, where Malcolm was assassinated on February 21, 1965. New York, February 21, 1996. AP Photo/Rosario Esposito. BOTTOM: The Black Power movement was international. Indian Dalits organized the Dalit Panthers in the 1970s. One of their influences was B.R. Ambedkar (on poster, far right), a prominent Dalit crusader. World Dignity Rally, Haryana State, India, 2004. AP Photo/Gurinder Osan.

Black Power salute in front of the Ferguson police headquarters. Ferguson, Missouri, 2014. © Charles Easterling/Demotix/Corbis.

The continued resonance, fifty years later, of the Black Power movement can be seen in this demonstration protesting the killing of Mario Woods and Alex Nieto by the San Francisco police. San Francisco, 2016. © Steve Rhodes/Demotix/Corbis.

Pennsylvania. Both were organized by the BPP.

The UFAFC took place in July 1969 and at least four thousand delegates attended, representing a diverse activist community of African Americans, Latinos, Asian Americans, and Native Americans. More than three hundred organizations from various parts of the United States participated, including groups such as the Young Lords, YPO, Red Guard, AIM, SDS, and Peace and Freedom Party. The purpose of the conference was to construct a united front of all communities and organizations struggling for self-determination under the banner of solidarity.

A representative of Chicago's Rainbow Coalition, Bill "Preacherman" Fesperman, of the YPO, participated in the UFAFC. He joined Jeff Jones of SDS, the Panthers' Elaine Brown and Don Cox, lawyers Bill Knustler and Charles Garry, activist Ron Dellums, and others on the panel titled "Political Prisoners and Political Freedom." In an attempt to quell the tension between SDS and the Panthers, Jeff Jones used his discussion time to outline the two groups' ideological similarities. He advocated that the student movement on college campuses be intricately linked to the liberation struggle of black and brown people, both domestically and abroad. He insisted that Panthers allow SDS to work in coalition with the Party because SDS wanted the student movement to encompass "the working class movement with support for the right of self-determination." He believed that SDS's involvement had to incorporate "over increased struggle, over increased militancy, over increased alliance, alliances with the working class, with the colonized people, the people oppressed by U.S. imperialism and fascism."[10] What came out of the conference was the National Committees to Combat Fascism (NCCF), which advocated for local community control of police and legal teams to defend political prisoners. By April of 1970, there were at least eighteen NCCF chapters in service around the country.[11]

The RPCC brought together between ten thousand and fifteen thousand people in Philadelphia in September 1970. Delegates from an array of organizations such as AIM, the Brown Berets, the Young Lords, I Wor Kuen, SDS, and others gathered to write a new constitution that represented a united vision of a more just and free society. Some examples from this highly progressive constitution are: an international bill of rights, a redistribution of the world's wealth, a ban on the production and use of genocidal weapons, a police control board, an end to the draft, prohibition of spending more than 10 percent of the nation's budget on the military and police, universities' resources made available to people's needs worldwide, free medical care, rights and protections for gay people, rights and protections for women, and an end to male supremacy.[12] In essence, the constitution was representative of the kind of people, communities, and organizations that created racial and class coalitions to reshape their realities. These U.S. citizens not only called for a new nation but a new world that embraced solidarity, liberation, and tolerance for difference and diversity.

Emory Douglas working on the Black Panther Party newspaper, which was used as a tool for education. Members were asked to read, discuss, and evaluate the Party's work as presented in the paper. Douglas said that it pushed some people to learn how to read. Oakland, 1969. © Stephen Shames.

CHAPTER 3

Black Power and "Education for Liberation"

Russell Rickford

n the era of Black Power, African Americans ceased to be "Negroes" and became something far more affirming and complicated: "Afro American," and, ultimately, "black." This conversion captured the hope and determination at the heart of the contemporary revolution in education. A host of grassroots black educational struggles unfolded between the mid-1960s and the mid-1970s. Schools and other sites of learning provided the critical terrain for battles over black studies, community control, and African American identity. Black Americans looked to education as a vehicle for social and political transformation and as a means of redefining themselves and reconstructing their lives. The creativity and fervor of Black Power educational efforts belie accounts of a fundamentally counterproductive movement. At the same time, the diversity of such campaigns calls into question something most Black Power proponents accepted as an article of faith: the existence of a single, cohesive "black community."

African Americans have regarded education as a path to liberation since the days of slavery, when some risked severe punishment and even death to learn to read and write. During the 1860s, in the aftermath of the Civil War, former slaves "clamored for schooling,"

one historian notes, "because they viewed it simultaneously as a rejection of their enslaved past and as a means of power and respect in the postemancipation world." As African Americans moved into the twentieth century, facing Jim Crow segregation in the South and other forms of structural racism in the North, they continued to view schools as key instruments in the quest for dignity and autonomy. *Brown v. Board of Education,* the 1954 Supreme Court ruling outlawing state-sanctioned segregation in public schools, vindicated the long fight against separate and unequal education. In their drive for freedom, however, African Americans infused the decision with far more emancipatory meaning than conservative, Cold War America could have anticipated.[1]

A mass black insurgency arose in the latter half of the 1950s, imbued with valuable experience from earlier struggles. African Americans in the North and the South escalated crusades for full citizenship. As crucial mechanisms of social advancement, schools were essential to their cause. The grassroots black assault on segregation gathered momentum in the early to mid-1960s. Massive boycotts and demonstrations for "quality integrated education" took place in many of the urban centers to which growing numbers of African Americans migrated. While the

" BY THE LATE 1960S INSISTENCE ON BLACK AUTONOMY AND INTERNAL DEVELOPMENT OF AFRICAN AMERICAN COMMUNITIES HAD RESHAPED BLACK EDUCATIONAL OUTLOOKS. "

1964 Civil Rights Act demolished the legal edifice of Jim Crow, no law or policy fundamentally transformed the educational experiences of the millions of African Americans who were relegated to substandard facilities. Many inner-city schools serving children of color remained grim symbols of neglect. Abandoned by white families as they fled the urban core, such institutions were often overcrowded, underfunded, and full of outdated materials and equipment. Acknowledging the scale of decay, the *Washington Post* declared in 1967 that "the collapse of public education in Washington is now evident."[2]

The 1966 cry for "Black Power" initiated a new phase of militant organizing. African

Malcolm X Liberation University. Howard Fuller/Owusu Sadaukai stated that the objective of the school was "to provide a framework within which black education can become relevant to the needs of the black community and the struggle for black liberation." The school closed in 1973 for lack of funding. Photograph by Bill Boyarsky. Courtesy North Carolina Collection, Durham County Library.

Americans continued to resist the indignities of segregation, even as they drew energy and direction from resurgent demands for black self-determination and self-definition. While desegregation was widely seen as a route to empowerment, few African Americans considered it an end in itself. The primary objective was high-quality education, not racial intermingling. Black people envisioned just and equitable integration, not a one-sided affair in which they sacrificed convenience, comfort, and culture for the sake of decent textbooks and modern facilities. Still, faith in the ameliorative power of desegregation began to wane or was eclipsed by mounting ambivalence, especially as white flight from public education and urban centers accelerated and other forms of segregationist opposition intensified. "I don't think it's a question of us forgetting integration," one African American parent-activist observed in 1968. "Integration has forgotten about us."[3]

In the 1970s, Supreme Court decrees first expanded then narrowed the scope of desegregation reform. Large-scale busing as a means of diversifying schools further alienated some African Americans, particularly those whose children were shuttled to distant and hostile districts. Black people who had never equated quality education with integration objected to the branding of black schools as sites of "racial isolation." They rejected the notion, embedded within the language and logic of *Brown v. Board,* that the absence of white students damaged the psyches and academic potential of African American children. Meanwhile renewed emphasis on black group identity expanded visions of the social and political functions of schooling. Black nationalism was a salient aspect of African American life and culture, not simply a result of frustration or disaffection. Its revitalization was an organic development in the evolution of black educational thought. Black nationalist themes of racial pride and awareness enriched the quest for dignified American citizenship and provided a wellspring of political action.

By the late 1960s insistence on black autonomy and internal development of African American communities had reshaped black educational outlooks. African Americans redoubled efforts to cultivate a bold and uncompromising sense of peoplehood and to determine for themselves "who we are and shall be." The quest for redemptive education transcended the simplistic "integration—separation" dichotomy and challenged some of the core values of

American schooling. Many contemporary African American educational struggles sought radical reform rather than incremental change, group progress rather than individual freedom, humanism rather than materialism, and political engagement rather than mere social mobility. They were guided not by technocratic ideals, but by expansive visions of democratic transformation. They included cosmopolitan and internationalist perspectives, a reflection of revived interest in African cultural heritage and Third World movements. They generated such ferment that one intellectual suggested that American education had entered a "pre-revolutionary" period.[4]

Rising aspirations for black cultural and political independence led to a flourishing of African American educational organizations. The late 1960s witnessed the birth

———

At Duke University, African American students staged a sit-in and study-in in 1967 to protest the use of segregated facilities by student groups. In February 1969, students of the Afro-American Society occupied the main administration building. Their action became known as the "Allen Building Takeover." They demanded the creation of a black studies department, the right to have a black student union, increased admission of black students, and adequate financial aid. Allen Building Study-in, November 13, 1967. Allen Building Takeover Collection, David M. Rubenstein Rare Books & Manuscript Library, Duke University.

of the short-lived National Association of Afro-American Educators and the African Heritage Studies Association, which survives to this day. Other outfits stressing black solidarity and self-help appeared, from the Black Caucus of the American Federation of Teachers to the more moderate Concerned Black Parents, Inc. Formed in 1964, New York City's Negro Teachers Association renamed itself the Afro-American Teachers' Association in 1967. During a Crisis in Our Schools Conference that year, its members demanded smaller class sizes, parent assistants in inner-city classrooms, and textbooks featuring black characters and "situations which are found in Afro-American communities."[5]

While the surge of black organizational life proved deeply influential, some of the most powerful educational struggles were decentralized and largely unstructured.

Malcolm X Liberation University opened in Durham, North Carolina, in October 1969 and moved to Greensboro in 1970. Its leader was Howard Fuller (right), who changed his name to Owusu Sadaukai. Photograph by Harold Cooper, Herald-Sun Newspaper. Courtesy North Carolina Collection, Durham County Library.

ERICKA HUGGINS
Freedom

I was born in Washington, DC. In 1963 I was fifteen when I heard about the March on Washington for Jobs and Freedom. Against my mother's wishes I took the city bus to the march that day in August. When I got to the grounds of Capitol Hill, there were thousands and thousands of people. I was awed by the joy and tenderness in the ocean of brown faces. One after another, speakers stepped forward with their words. Their presence was so much more important to me than what they said.

At a certain point one of my favorite people stepped forward.

As she stood on center stage, the ocean roared. Ms. Lena Horne, singer, actress, and spokesperson for the rights of poor and black people, sang the word *FREEDOM*. The two powerful syllables lifted into the air and seemed to land softly on the raised heads and hands of the marchers.

As Lena sang, the syllables entered my heart and settled, and I became very still. From the depths of my being, a vow arose: "I will serve people for the rest of my life." Though I never forgot that moment on Capitol Hill, life unfolded in predictable ways for the next two years. I

finished high school and enrolled in Lincoln University, a historically black college, as one of the first fifteen women to integrate the campus. There, conversations led to actions to end apartheid in South Africa and to end the war in the streets of America and in Vietnam.

I had the privilege of hearing Stokely Carmichael and Charles Hamilton read chapters from their new book, *Black Power,* which created a conversation about *why we can't wait* to reclaim the power to determine the destiny of black and poor communities.

The concept of Black Power and the movement that followed did not arise outside of history; many people around the globe have been subjected to inhumane conditions. Throughout time the colonized and the enslaved have taken action to break the yoke of violent subjugation and break free of social and economic chains. Power based in personal

and structural greed is violent. Power based in love for humanity is sacred.

The political awakening on college campuses planted the seeds that blossomed into black and African studies, Chicano(a) studies, Native American studies, Asian American studies, and women's studies. Everything was moving. This grassroots movement led by young people was international. We were the generation that believed in the word "revolution," a complete structural transformation in society. We studied what was happening in Cuba, in Ghana and other countries in Africa, in Vietnam and all over Asia. In the United States a multigenerational united front that transcended culture, ethnicity, gender, class, immigrant status, sexual orientation, and ability coalesced against oppression.

Daily life in the communities we came from was the catalyst for a shift in consciousness on

campuses. At Lincoln University I met John Huggins. He was a great humanitarian and a loving, loyal friend, as well as a veteran and an activist. I loved him. One day in 1967 I sat in the Student Union Building, reading a *Ramparts* magazine article about the Black Panther Party for Self-Defense and the shooting and jailing of Huey P. Newton.

Together, John and I made the decision to drive to California to join the Black Panther Party and the Free Huey campaign. When we arrived in Los Angeles we searched the streets for the Black Panther Party (BPP) office. We joined in November 1967.

There was no job too big or small for us. As members, we sold the BPP newspaper, we raised money, we spoke to crowds and small groups, and we took care of each other. Alprentice "Bunchy" Carter and John became leaders of the Los Angeles chapter. Before John and I were introduced to Bobby Seale, co-founder

Contemporary black student revolts had no established national leader and followed no standard political formula. Yet they tested the social and ethical foundations of higher education. In the late 1960s and early 1970s, a wave of black student dissent struck colleges and universities nationwide. Galvanized by the freedom struggle, urban insurrections, Third World revolutions, the Vietnam War, and the political assassinations of the day, thousands of African American students rebelled against "a hopelessly white educational apparatus," undertaking what historian Lerone Bennett called "a painful and necessary labor of self-discovery."[6]

The new recruitment efforts of many institutions increased African American college enrollment, which in turn helped precipitate campus revolts. Politicized students of all colors recognized that universities were not pristine temples of wisdom, but, rather, guardians of the status quo and defenders of the prevailing values and dynamics of the broader society, from war and racism to economic inequality. For black students, many of whom and chairman of the BPP, we heard him speak about the brilliant vision of Huey Newton. I felt I was in the right place, at the right time, with the right people.

I knew that Merritt College, a two-year college in Oakland, was the birthplace of the BPP. Merritt was the college where community organizers Bobby and Huey met, eventually taking their message back to the community. The honest and vocal approach of the BPP captured the attention of a nation and inspired countless young people to come to California to join the fight for social justice.

The Ten-Point Program was the platform for the many community survival programs. Point seven, "We want an immediate end to police brutality," fostered the community patrols of police. With law books and guns, Huey, Bobby, and many other members actively patrolled the police. By patrolling those who unjustly patrolled us, we modeled one way to reclaim the power to determine the destiny of our communities.

In response to black men with guns, J. Edgar Hoover, then FBI director, pronounced the BPP "the single greatest threat to the internal security of the United States." In the years that followed Hoover's statement, many Party members were routinely surveilled and jailed—and some were killed. The FBI worked in collusion with local police departments to "neutralize" the BPP and the human rights movement. The project created to carry out these illegal, clandestine activities was called the Counterintelligence Program, COINTELPRO.

On January 17, 1969, John and Bunchy were killed on the UCLA campus.

The BPP was named the Vanguard of the Revolution. Groups representing every community used BPP strategies and tools such as the Ten-Point Program and the community newspaper as the framework for organizing in their own communities. Many groups in communities of color and poor white communities throughout the United States were organizing: Brown Berets, Young Lords Party, Young Patriots, I Wor Kuen, the American Indian Movement. The poverty and inequities in these communities made us allies.

The earliest BPP survival programs transformed and empowered communities. If the government could not feed, clothe, and provide health care for its people, we created a community-based free program to do it. The Free Breakfast for Children Program, the People's Free Medical Clinics, the Oakland Community School (OCS), the Seniors Against a Fearful Environment, the Busing to Prisons Program, and many others met the needs of thousands throughout the United States. Women and men of the BPP, supported by volunteers from the community, educators, nutritionists, doctors, hailed from marginalized communities, this epiphany was especially jarring. Some adopted a defiant political outlook, openly identifying with the most oppressed elements of society while striving to make higher education "relevant" to black liberation. According to one San Jose State University professor, the time had passed when degreed "Negroes" could simply escape to Baldwin Hills, a posh Los Angeles neighborhood, to "eat pickles and hors d'oeuvres and watch the riots on color TV."[7]

Black campus dissidents attempted to reconstruct the American university. They pressed for "black studies"—a populist reformulation of the old "Negro Studies" concept—as a necessary corrective for curricula that presented white, Western civilization as "the universal yardstick of human experience." They demanded larger black enrollments, more African American faculty and staff, and greater financial and cultural resources for students of color, mounting demonstrations and collaborating with other student groups to achieve their goals. A groundbreaking struggle at San Francisco State College produced the nation's first black studies program and "black student union." As James P. Garrett, a leader of the campaign, recalls, "The idea was to politicize the growing consciousness into a formation of a union. It was not simply an alliance or an association, but a union, a coming together of a broad base of black people."[8]

Students at historically black colleges and universities launched some of the earliest and most influential rebellions. The 1968 occupation of an administration building at Howard University in Washington, DC, preceded

nurses, and students, sustained these programs.

Point five of the Ten-Point Program emphasized the need to provide an education that, among other things, taught African American and poor people a sense of self and their true place in history. The longest standing community survival program of the Black Panther Party was the Oakland Community School, but the educational programs of the BPP started long before that. In 1967 Huey Newton and Bobby Seale taught youth in San Francisco Bay Area public high schools. In 1969, in cities where there were BPP chapters, liberation schools, staffed by BPP members, opened in storefronts, churches, and homes.

In 1970, David Hilliard, then BPP chief of staff, opened a full day liberation school in Oakland called the Children's House. In 1971 this school was renamed the Intercommunal Youth Institute (IYI). Under the direction of Brenda Bay, the IYI served the sons and daughters of BPP members and nearby families in the Fruitvale area of Oakland. It maintained a school program and dormitory for fifty children. In September of 1973 the school became known as Oakland Community School. Its doors opened at 6118 International Boulevard in East Oakland. The school's enrollment quickly blossomed to one hundred fifty children, plus a waiting list.

From 1973 until 1982 OCS—directed by myself, assisted by Donna Howell—was a focal point serving the extended community and its children. It became an identifiable and replicable educational model. Educators and staff of the OCS, Black Panther Party members, and former Oakland, San Francisco, and Berkeley Unified School District teachers held the school philosophy that children at OCS "will learn how, not what, to think."

The school provided quality, tuition-free education. The Educational Opportunities Corporation (EOC), the school's nonprofit sponsor, received private donations and grants for funding from city and county resources and foundations and the California State Department of Education. Parents donated their time and skills in and outside the classroom. Students were admitted, from a waiting list, on a first-come, first-served basis. A student's ethnicity, gender, economic class, or ability was never a factor for entrance or retention. Due to its East Oakland location, OCS students were 90 percent African American. About 10 percent of the students were Mexican American, Asian American, and European American students.

Former students remember the OCS experience as a happy and transformative one. Their day began with a ten-minute exercise program. Breakfast was followed by a short, school-wide interactive check-in that

The Harlem Liberation School launched by Malcolm X's Organization of Afro-American Unity in 1964 inspired "liberation schools" in various states. Black Panther Party Liberation School, San Francisco, 1969. © Bettmann/Corbis/ AP Images.

preceded morning classes. A nutritious lunch was provided at midday, followed by ten minutes of meditation. In the afternoon, classes continued for the older children while the youngest ones rested. Dinner concluded the day. The student-centered curriculum included math, English, Spanish, science, history, geography, creative writing, physical education, art, music, and drama classes.

The students remember the OCS teachers and staff with great love: Lorene Banks, Melvin Dickson, Haven Henderson, Vivette Miller, Lula Hudson, Gayle Dickson, James Mott, Rodney Gillead,

Pamela Ward, Joe Abron, Joan Kelley, Linda Dunson, Amar Casey, Steve McCutchen, Tommye Williams, Jody Weaver, Norma Mtume, Carol Granison, Charles Moffitt, Frank Kellum, Joan Kelley, Adrienne Humphrey, and many more.

Great poets, artists, and activists including Rosa Parks, Cesar Chavez, Maya Angelou, James Baldwin, Sun Ra, and Richard Pryor visited and showered the students with their empowering and loving presence. Educators and graduate students visited as guest teachers and interns; many returned to their own state or country to replicate the school.

The value of the BPP education programs does not rest solely with the OCS. Its legacy lives in the hearts of the children, now adults, who were taught then; it continues to live in the generations of children they touch now.

Panther schools were designed to sharpen the political consciousness of children while fostering a vigorous critique of the majority culture. Chicano, Nat ive American, and Puerto Rican groups followed the model, establishing their own alternative schools. Panther children at school, Oakland, 1972. © Stephen Shames.

LEFT: *Liberation school translated the internationalist and anticapitalist principles of the Marxist-Leninist ideals into simple slogans and themes. Black Panther Party School, San Francisco, 1972. © Stephen Shames. MIDDLE: Responding to the needs of poor communities, Panther schools provided meals to the students. Black Panther member Bill Whitfield, serving free breakfast to children in Kansas City. 1969. AP Photo/William P. Straeter. RIGHT: Students of the Liberation School loading trucks with Black Panther Party newspapers, 1969. © Bettmann/Corbis.*

" INCREASINGLY, HOWEVER, AFRICAN AMERICAN PARENTS RESISTED THE NOTION THAT POOR AND WORKING-CLASS BLACK YOUTHS WERE BEARERS OF CULTURAL DEFICIENCIES THAT REQUIRED CORRECTION—A DOCTRINE OF INFERIORITY THAT DETROIT'S INNER CITY PARENTS COUNCIL CONDEMNED AS 'NAZI-LIKE.' "

historic student takeovers at Columbia and Cornell. Howard protestors sought curricular reform, autonomy in student affairs, and an end to the institution's cultural isolation from surrounding poor and working-class African American neighborhoods. "We wanted Howard to make a statement about its commitment to the black community, to the welfare of the black community," Adrienne Manns, an organizer of the strike, later remembered. Revolts also flared at Jackson State College, Southern University, Fisk University, and other black schools. The repudiation of intellectual detachment and the desire for meaningful engagement fueled the concept of the "Black University." Rooted in the search for a model of higher learning that could serve "the total black community," the ideal helped inspire several activist organizations, including the Student Organization for Black Unity and the Institute of the Black World, an Atlanta think tank.[9]

Though university upheavals seized headlines, student rebellions also erupted on scores of high school campuses. Thousands of African American secondary school students rallied in Philadelphia, Chicago, New York, and other cities, demanding black history classes, more black teachers and administrators, and, in some cases, Swahili courses, official celebration of Malcolm X Day, and job counseling centers. African American parents and activists launched parallel campaigns. In 1968, one hundred black residents of coastal South Carolina gathered in Frogmore, a rural community on St. Helena Island, for a Citizens Conference on Education. Convened by a mattress factory foreman, the meeting addressed longstanding injustices, including the refusal of district administrators to furnish black parents with school budgets, and the official practice of dumping garbage behind the lunchroom of an African American senior high. While education workshops at major Black Power conferences drew bigger crowds, the Frogmore assemblage—which condemned "Negro" as "a white man's word" and accused district officials of selecting principals for black schools who would do the bidding of "the white power structure"—touched many of the themes that framed those larger gatherings.[10]

The quest for social relevance in primary and secondary schooling inspired a rejection of some of the premises of "compensatory" education. Theories of social disadvantage

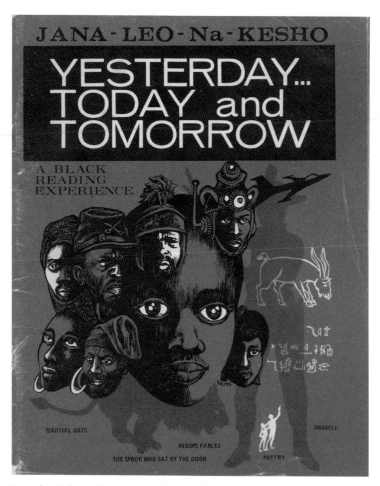

Yesterday, Today and Tomorrow: A Black Reading Experience. *The seventy-eight-page book was published by the Uhuru Sasa School in Brooklyn. It included texts by the assassinated Congo prime minister Patrice Lumumba, BAM poet Sonia Sanchez, SNCC/BPP activists James Forman and H. Rap Brown, as well as martial arts coloring pages. 1972. Jean Blackwell Hutson Research and Reference Division, Schomburg Center for Research in Black Culture, The New York Public Library.*

continued to govern the education of many children of color. Increasingly, however, African American parents resisted the notion that poor and working-class black youths were bearers of cultural deficiencies that required correction—a doctrine of inferiority that Detroit's Inner City Parents Council condemned as "Nazi-like." Like other classroom injustices, from racist systems of academic "tracking" to the discriminatory use of suspensions and expulsions, such "thinly disguised" bigotry deepened African American resentment. Black educators, artists, intellectuals, and children's book authors launched counteroffensives, affirming the distinctiveness and beauty of black dialects, learning styles, and community values. They celebrated the ingenuity, resilience, and soulfulness of African American life, attempting to arm black youngsters with a sense of cultural integrity.[11] These and other efforts suggested that the most liberating impulses in black education stemmed from autonomous African American activities, rather than from the top-down reforms of policymakers or administrators.

The popular thrust for self-determination helped propel the community control movement, an attempt by parents of color to participate directly in the governance of neighborhood schools. Brooklyn's impoverished Ocean Hill–Brownsville section provided the central battleground in the struggle for educational home rule. Embracing a do-it-yourself approach after years of what they viewed as the miseducation of their children, black and Puerto Rican parents in 1967 helped bring about the partial decentralization of New York City's Board of Education. Along with demonstration sites in Harlem and the Lower East Side, the independent Ocean Hill–Brownsville district briefly emerged as a nexus of educational innovation, participatory democracy, and political expression.

Locally elected members of the Ocean Hill–Brownsville board hired some of the city's first minority principals, revamped curricula, and greatly increased parent involvement in the daily functions of area schools. Preston Wilcox, a Harlem organizer, argued that community control occasioned "a shift within the black community from the position of aggrieved complainant to that of the articulate spokesman on behalf of one's own interest." The Ocean Hill–Brownsville experiment attracted an assortment of educators, activists, and ideologues. Though the project reflected multiple political tendencies, black nationalists played a significant leadership role. Among the more radical subplots in the saga of the district was a fruitless attempt by the separatist Republic of New Afrika to encourage local residents to secede from the United States. "If [black] people in Ocean Hill–Brownsville, and anywhere else, really want local control," one militant declared, "the only way to achieve it is outside the U.S. federal system."[12]

A more mundane desire to see their children properly educated motivated the thousands of parents in other major cities who also sought community control. Even African American nuns demanded self-determination for predominantly black Catholic schools. While some of these campaigns led to restructured school boards and the hiring of more personnel of color, none

forced a permanent redistribution of authority to poor and working-class neighborhoods. The Ocean Hill–Brownsville struggle itself ended in defeat. Disputes over the extent of the independent board's powers ignited massive teacher strikes in 1968, and the local district was effectively dissolved the following year. Yet amid the endless marches and picket-line confrontations, political consciousness expanded. Community control battles suggested that inner cities were suppressed political territories, not just slums. Black parents and workers were activists who had seized power from remote bureaucrats, not passive victims of urban decay. Education was now an arena for grassroots attempts to reimagine and transform, rather than merely escape, "the ghetto."

The "build where you are" ethic and spirit of experimentation spawned an array of alternative community education models. This category included scores of formal and informal self-help ventures dedicated to the intergenerational transfer of knowledge and culture. Black Power visions of emancipatory learning crystallized in "street academies" for dropouts and at-risk youths; independent daycare centers run by civil rights veterans; black YMCAs offering Swahili and African American history classes; and independent bookstores that hosted lectures, workshops, and study groups. These small, creative institutions were among the most "overlooked" Black Power formations, but they played crucial roles in the intellectual and cultural development of people of color, especially as public programs in urban centers fell victim to cutbacks. Often created and run by neighborhood residents on behalf of local populations, alternative models rooted curricula in the lives and experiences of black people while giving programmatic structure to Black Power ideals.

The new public and semipublic prototypes included the Freedom School annex of Washington, DC.'s Eastern High School. The annex opened in 1968 after black students, angered by racial disparities in public school funding, organized as the Modern Strivers and began fighting for a school of their own. They gained support from several foundations and received permission to

" LIKE OTHER RADICAL ESTABLISH-MENTS TIED TO CONTEMPORARY MOVEMENTS ... PANTHER SCHOOLS WERE DESIGNED TO SHARPEN THE POLITICAL CONSCIOUSNESS OF POOR AND WORKING-CLASS CHILDREN WHILE FOSTERING A VIGOROUS CRI-TIQUE OF THE MAJORITY CULTURE. "

operate a student-run satellite in a church across the street from Eastern. There they organized elective courses, earning academic credit for studying "Third World history" and other subjects while continuing to take required classes at Eastern. Freedom School's mission, one of its young founders maintained, was to "scrape clean from our minds and hearts" the cultural and political residue of slavery.[13]

Ventures like the Eastern High annex built upon the civil rights movement's tradition of establishing independent freedom schools to critique the dominant society and maintain the education of youngsters during boycotts and other protest campaigns. In the mid- to late 1960s, however, "liberation" replaced "freedom" as the definitive moniker for radical, autonomous enterprises. Black Power militants opened "liberation schools" in Nashville, Tennessee, and Jackson, Mississippi, inspired in part by the Harlem liberation school that Malcolm X's Organization of Afro-American Unity had launched in 1964. Radical intellectual Angela Y. Davis later operated a Marxist-oriented liberation school associated with the Student Nonviolent Coordinating Committee's Los Angeles office.[14] Such efforts reflected the freedom struggle's growing emphasis on forming parallel structures to expose the deficiencies of mainstream institutions.

The most famous liberation schools belonged to the Black Panther Party. Like other radical establishments tied to contemporary movements—including American Indian "survival schools," Chicano "heritage academies," and the schools created by the Puerto Rican Young Lords, Panther schools were designed to sharpen the political consciousness of poor and working-class children while fostering a vigorous critique of the majority culture. Free, part-time classes were held in churches, housing projects, and other sites in dozens of African American neighborhoods across the country. The schools were one of several "survival programs" initiated by the Panthers in 1969 to address the everyday needs of underserved black populations and to offset the collapse of social services in urban centers. Liberation school classes translated internationalist and anticapitalist principles into simple slogans and themes. They served all ages, providing wholesome meals and attempting to hone academic skills while passing to the next generation "the means for waging the struggle."[15]

By the early 1970s, the rich political fusion of the Black Arts Movement, cultural and revolutionary nationalism, and Pan-Africanism had spawned another set of autonomous ventures. The new generation of "Pan-African nationalist" establishments included multi-purpose venues such as Chicago's Affro-Arts Theater, which offered youth classes in everything from Swahili to dance.[16] Dozens of full-time, Pan-African nationalist schools also appeared. Known as "independent black institutions," these enterprises shared the Black Panther aims of exposing "the true nature of this decadent American society" and nurturing the future vanguard of black liberation. However, while Panther schools reformulated Marxist-Leninist ideals, Pan-African nationalist institutions stressed African cultural identity, adopting the "We Are an African People" concept as their political and pedagogical foundation.

The private academies were founded by young activist-intellectuals who had witnessed firsthand the limitations of campus struggles, desegregation battles, and community control campaigns. These figures viewed the creation of parallel institutions "by, for, and of" black people as the next critical stage of struggle. By 1970 about sixty such ventures, from preschools to postsecondary establishments, had appeared in urban centers nationwide.[17] They subsisted on modest tuition fees, donations, private grants, and antipoverty funds, occupying storefronts and serving mainly poor and working-class African American children and young adults.

The schools flourished in the early to mid-1970s amid the heyday and denouement of contemporary black nationalist and Pan-Africanist activity, contributing to what historian Peniel E. Joseph characterizes as a reinvigoration or "second wave" of community-based Black Power organizing.[18] They included college-level establishments such as Malcolm X Liberation University in Greensboro, North Carolina, and the Center for Black Education in Washington, DC. Most of the academies were primary and secondary institutions, including Brooklyn's Uhuru Sasa Shule; African Free School in Newark, New Jersey; Philadelphia's Freedom Library Day School; New Concept Development Center of Chicago; Columbus, Ohio's Umoja Sasa Shule; Ahidiana Work/Study Center in New Orleans; the Learning House and Pan-African Work Center of Atlanta;

and Nairobi Day School of East Palo Alto, California.

Pan-African nationalist schools were designed to revolutionize culture. They strove to "re-Africanize" black Americans, animating social and political traits that their operators saw as consistent with both positive African traditions and contemporary anti-imperialist struggles. Founders of the institutions believed black children needed an alternative value system that could free them from internalized stigma while orienting them toward the worldwide struggle of African people. Instructors stressed "nation-building skills" as well as academic mastery. Students studied martial arts, postcolonial theory, and outdoor survival techniques along with more conventional subjects. The objective was to create a devoted leadership corps that might someday participate in genuine nation-building campaigns, either on the African continent or in the United States.

Even within African American communities, the idea of "teaching blackness from door to door" was not widely understood. "Many folks think all you do is to put up some pictures of Dr. King, Malcolm, and eat soul food for lunch," one proprietor of an independent black institution complained. The reality was more complex. Pan-African nationalist educators employed a host of techniques to foster communalism and "an undying love for all African people." Songs and recitations accompanied daily rituals, from mealtime ceremonies to spirited marches in and out of the *shule*. In many institutions, "Praise the Red, Black, and Green" was a familiar refrain:

> Praise the red, the black and the green
> Brothers and Sisters we are being redeemed
> Open up your eyes and see
> We're on our way to being free
> Because red is for the blood that we shed
> Black is for the race, that's us
> And the green is for the land, uh huh
> So the Black man can take his rightful place.[19]

Emphasis on "African restoration" inspired other practices. At Shule Ya Watoto ("School for Children") on Chicago's West Side, students were given African names for use

" AS BASES FOR COMMUNITY DEVELOPMENT AND ACTIVISM, THE ACADEMIES ORGANIZED HEALTH CLINICS, URBAN VEGETABLE GARDENS, COOPERATIVES, AND DRUG AND PRISON PROGRAMS WHILE PLAYING A LEADING ROLE IN AFRICAN LIBERATION DAY RALLIES AND OTHER ANTICOLONIAL AND ANTIRACIST CAUSES. "

in the classroom. Watoto director Hannibal Afrik (Harold E. Charles), a longtime teacher and community activist, insisted that the renaming process generated "positive self-concept." Thus in 1972, Armon became "Jahali," Sheritha became "Maisha," and Christopher became "Chaka," at least within the walls of the school.[20] However, the activities of Pan-African nationalist institutions were not limited to such "re-identification" exercises. The schools helped cultivate a vibrant alternative public sphere, maintaining small libraries, periodicals, and bookstores, and sponsoring festivals, concerts, radio programs, and Kwanzaa ceremonies. As bases for community development and activism, the academies organized health clinics, urban vegetable gardens, cooperatives, and drug and prison programs while playing a leading role in African Liberation Day rallies and other anticolonial and antiracist causes.

Pan-African nationalist institutions were frequently accused of indoctrination. The schools, which generally enrolled between twenty-five and two hundred fifty students, never represented a mass movement. Many of their organizers romanticized African

culture and overestimated the value of identity reorientation as a weapon against structural racism. Yet the establishments creatively reinterpreted the old Nation of Islam theme of personal reconstruction and collective rebirth. Their founders hoped to influence rather than abandon public education in African American neighborhoods. Independent black institutions represented a "dual strategy"—the attempt to restructure inner cities by gaining control of existing social organs while forming radical, alternative structures. In many ways, the schools reflected a broader, Third World commitment to "transforming the educational system inherited from the colonizers."[21]

From the perspective of the early twenty-first century, Black Power visions of education for liberation appear largely unfulfilled. Crusades to eliminate the gulf between the campus and "the street," to convert black schools and colleges into citadels of democracy, and to construct a vast network of thriving, alternative institutions, fell well short of those goals. The militant campaigns of the late 1960s and 1970s remain absent from most narratives of the African American freedom struggle's decisive battles. Yet Black Power educational endeavors provide concrete evidence that the movement was far more than a proliferation of frustrated rhetoric. Indeed, the impulses behind such efforts—the need to emancipate consciousness, to reclaim the past, and to reassert the humanity and dignity of the oppressed—are alive today. As radical educator Doxey A. Wilkerson noted during the Black Power era, "It is not the education of black men and women that will achieve their liberation; it is the liberation of black Americans that will assure their effective education."[22]

THE AFFRO-ARTS THEATER

3947 SOUTH DREXEL BOULEVARD — CHICAGO, ILL. 60637 — WA 4-2140

THE AFFRO-ARTS THEATER FREE BLACK COMMUNITY CULTURAL COLLEGE

One of the most important functions of the Affro-Arts Theater is the enlightenment of our own community and to awaken the multitude of talents which now lay dormant within these boundries. In harmony with this above stated goal is this important extension of our performing theater, the FREE BLACK COMMUNITY CULTURAL COLLEGE.
The only investment required from the students is interest, sincerity and time. We therefore extend a cordial invitation to all black people to avail themselves to any or to all of the classes we offer, and we sincerely hope that this will contribute to a stronger and to an enlightened black future. The revised schedule is:

DAY	TIME	SUBJECT	INSTRUCTOR
Monday	7:00 PM	Black Womanhood	Varied
Tuesday	6:00 PM	Swahili	Noah Ngatho
Wednesday	4:00 PM	Dance Class	Blackburn Dancers
	7:00 PM	Black Manhood	
Thursday	7:00 PM	Dramatic & Song Workshop	Bro Spencer Jackson Sr.
Saturday	10:00 AM	Beginning Swahili	Noah Ngatho
	11:00 AM	Writers Workshop	Varied
	12:00 PM	Advanced Swahili	Noah Ngatho
	1:00 PM	African Fundamentalism	James Davis
	3:00 PM.	Dance Workshop	Blackburn Dancers
	3:00 PM	Conga Class	Pharaohs
	3:00 PM	Contemporary African Affairs	Ruwa Chiri
	5:00 PM	Drama Workshop	Harold Lee Van Jackson
	5:00 PM	Self Defense Class (Karate)	Russell Brown
Sunday	1:00 PM	Hebrew Class	Bro Napthali
	1:00 PM	Art Workshop	Bro Berry
	3:00 PM	Arabic Class	M. Bliebel
	5:00 PM	Drum Class	Pharaohs

CLASSES IN ALL INSTRUMENTS OFFERED ON AN INDIVIDUAL BASIS UPON

STUDENTS ARRANGEMENT WITH INSTRUCTOR (at theater).

Chicago's Affro-Arts Theater opened in 1967. It featured plays, dance, and music and was also a meeting place for Black Power activists. The theater's Free Black Community Cultural College offered various classes. Photographs and Prints Division, Schomburg Center for Research in Black Culture, The New York Public Library.

On August 18, 1970, Angela Davis was the third woman to be placed on the FBI's Ten Most Wanted Fugitives list. She was charged with supplying the guns that George Jackson's seventeen-year-old brother, Jonathan, used in a failed attempt to free three black prisoners in August 1970. Her trial was one of the most famous court cases in the United States and was followed throughout the world. Individuals and organizations created items to wear in support of her freedom and innocence. *Oakland, 1972. © Stephen Shames.*

CHAPTER 4

America Means Prison: Political Prisoners in the Age of Black Power

Dan Berger

The Black Power movement was made and unmade through encounters with the criminal justice system, especially the prison. That prisons would contribute to the unmaking of a social movement seems self-evident. After all, they are a combination of structural boredom and physical violence. Prisons are, by definition, the most repressive aspect of society, places where state power can be its most ferocious. They are far from urban population centers, surrounded by thick walls and barbed wire, and patrolled by heavily armed guards. Prisons are supposed to house "dangerous" people and leave those in the broader public at a further distance from incarcerated people.

Thus it is rather remarkable that black activists in the 1960s and 1970s used their experience of prisons and the wider criminal justice system to craft a globally minded Black Power movement. Black Power activists described the criminal justice system—including police, prosecutors, and prisons—as a central element of the racism and urban inequality that they so vehemently opposed. Prisons were especially central to activists' efforts as they drew on their own experiences of confinement to indict a broader system of white supremacy. Many of the movement's strategists, theoreticians, and foot soldiers spent time in jail or prison. For some, prison was the consequence of their organizing. For others, it was where they joined and contributed to the Black Power movement. Prison was both a recruiting ground and a staging ground for Black Power.[1]

Black Power engaged the prison experience of working-class black people, especially men, who were disproportionately imprisoned. Indeed, though the overall prison population fell during the 1960s, the rates of black and Latino incarceration relative to white incarceration rose, as did the overall numbers of black and Latino prisoners. Imprisonment shaped Black Power from beginning to end: many of the people who joined organizations such as the Nation of Islam or the Black Panther Party had been incarcerated as juveniles or young adults. Others joined the movement while in prison. And efforts to free or spare political radicals from imprisonment—including Huey Newton, George Jackson, Angela Davis, Joan Little, and dozens of others—catalyzed the Black Power movement on a global scale. Black political prisoners were internationally recognized spokespersons and symbols of resistance as campaigns to prevent people from

going to or staying in prison circulated the world. Black Power activists used the prison experience to indict American racism before a global audience.

Collectively, these activists became the voices for and shock troops of the Black Power movement—especially the Nation of Islam from the late 1950s to 1964, the Black Panther Party from 1966 to the early 1970s, and the Republic of New Afrika from 1971 onward. These organizations joined those that people formed inside of prisons, including the Black Guerrilla Family. Each of these organizations, along with several others that formed in this milieu, sought to challenge both the racism of American prisons and the "prison" of American racism

as experienced through police brutality, urban inequality, and foreign wars.

Black Power spread through a series of conflicts with the criminal justice system. The urban rebellions of 1963 to 1968 were often sparked by incidents of police brutality and saw thousands of people arrested. Over the next four years, black activists led a historic wave of rebellions inside American prisons. Following such uprisings, prisons became more restrictive. Activists resorted to study groups, escape attempts, newspapers, and legal appeals to challenge prison as both a metaphor for oppression and an example of it. But their efforts failed to transform society as they had hoped. Indeed, by the mid-1970s there was

growing bipartisan support for increasing the severity and length of sentences. Thus began the rise of mass incarceration that would disproportionately impact the youth who had been the base of the Black Power movement. Even so, the movement accomplished some stunning victories in its attempt to disentangle blackness from state violence.

THE PRISON OF RACISM, 1955–1965

Malcolm Little did not seem destined to change the world. The Nebraska native lost both his parents at a young age: his father was killed and his mother suffered an emotional breakdown. Shortly thereafter, fourteen-year-old Little was imprisoned in a detention home. In 1946, three months before his twenty-first birthday, Little was sentenced to serve between eight to ten years in prison as a result of a series of burglaries he committed with a small, interracial group of friends.

Within two years, he had joined the Nation of Islam (NOI) and adopted the surname of X. When he got out of prison in 1952, Malcolm X would go on to make the Nation of Islam the most significant forerunner of the Black Power movement and a vocal, if inconsistent, advocate of prisoner rights. The Nation of Islam had taken an interest in prisons after its leader, Elijah Muhammad, had been incarcerated for refusing to fight in World War II. Muhammad began recruiting prisoners after seeing that large numbers of black men, mostly southern migrants, were being arrested in Chicago, Detroit, Harlem, Los Angeles, and other major cities of the North.

Throughout the 1950s and early 1960s, the NOI developed a reputation inside American prisons for supporting the personal transformation and collective racial pride of its members. It offered a political explanation for black imprisonment, legal support for prisoners organizing for religious freedom, and a personal code of conduct for responding to confinement. The NOI supported a number of lawsuits against prison officials around the country, enabling NOI members to practice their faith.

By far the biggest boost to the NOI's efforts to recruit in prison was Malcolm X. The young minister and fiery orator did not shy away from his prison record. Rather, he saw it as emblematic of the racism that confined black people. "Don't be shocked when I say I was in prison," he often told audiences, rejecting the stigma of incarceration. "You're still in prison. That's what America means—prison." As part of the platform included in the NOI newspaper,

PANTHER RALLY

AMERICAN REVOLUTION # 2

HOTEL DIPLOMAT
108 WEST 43 ST.

MONDAY, SEPT. 15   8 PM

DONATION: $2.00

SPEAKERS

Black Panther Party   Young Patriots
Young Lords Organization

POETRY and MUSIC

FREE FILMS   FREE REFRESHMENTS

Dedicated to the people from the Black Panther Party NEW YORK   21

If you want to know a certain thing or a certain class of things directly, you must personally participate in the practical struggle to change reality, to change that thing or class of things, . . . only through   personal participation in the practical struggle to change reality can you uncover the heart of that thing or class of things and understand them.

Mao

In New York City, twenty-one Panthers were indicted on a series of specious charges in 1969. In May 1971, after forty-five minutes of jury deliberation, all defendants were acquitted. Although a vindication and victory of sorts, the lengthy time the Panthers spent in jail and the disruption of the trial had unsettled the Party and hampered some of its activities. Flyer for a Panther 21 rally organized by the BPP, the Young Patriots, and the Young Lords at the Hotel Diplomat in New York. Amistad Research Center.

———

Muhammad Speaks, Malcolm voiced a call to release Muslim prisoners. He echoed such sentiments in his bestselling autobiography, which described his incarceration as a turning point in his political evolution. The book became a staple among black prisoners, encouraging their literacy and social consciousness. Indeed, *The Autobiography of Malcolm X* stimulated other prisoners to tell their stories, and several prisoner autobiographies or books of letters appeared in the following years.

Malcolm X left the NOI in 1964 and was assassinated in 1965, just as urban revolts around the country seemed to demonstrate the black insurgency of which he spoke. Dissident black prisoners increasingly pinned their hopes to these new urban guerrillas. Between 1963 and 1968, hundreds of urban rebellions took place as a consequence of black dissatisfaction with a racial hierarchy most visibly characterized by structural unemployment and rampant police brutality. The biggest of these incidents—Watts in 1965, Detroit and Newark in 1967—caused millions of dollars of damage and resulted in dozens of deaths and hundreds of people imprisoned. But no city was immune to the spirit of black militancy and frustration. Paterson, a small industrial town in northern New Jersey, experienced an uprising in

1967 that saw insurgents raid the Plainfield Machine Company, a local gun manufacturer, and use the weapons to hold off police and the National Guard.

DEFENSE CAMPAIGNS GROW THE MOVEMENT, 1966–1971

Typically catalyzed by incidents of police violence, these uprisings bespoke lifetimes of frustration, marginalization, and hope. A variety of organizations formed in their wake, each attempting to harness the explosive energy of the riots. The organization best able to speak to young, educated, and underemployed people who participated in these uprisings was the Black Panther Party for Self-Defense (BPP). Huey P. Newton and Bobby Seale formed the Party in Oakland, California, in October 1966. Newton and Seale encapsulated the rise of black Oakland: born in the South, studying at the working-class Merritt College, well traveled in the field of black protest, and veterans of the two primary institutions that, as the old joke went, gave black men an education. Seale served in the military and Newton had been incarcerated as a juvenile in the California Youth Authority.

Borrowing from Malcolm X, the BPP's platform demanded "freedom for all Black men held in federal, state, county, and city prisons and jails," which was later amended to call for "the elimination of all prisons and jails in the U.S., and trial by a jury of peers for all persons charged with so-called crimes under the laws of this country."[2] Prisons influenced the daily work of what it meant to be a Black Panther. Members were expected to visit, write letters to, answer phone calls from, and generally raise awareness about the existence of the party's political prisoners. Further, Panthers were frequently arrested and jailed for selling the party newspaper, staging

"PERHAPS THE MOST IMMEDIATE REASON FOR THE BPP'S RAPID RISE OWED TO ITS SKILLFUL DEMANDS FOR THE FREEDOM OF BLACK POLITICAL PRISONERS—INCLUDING ITS OWN LEADERSHIP. BETWEEN 1967 AND 1972, THE ORGANIZATION WAGED A VARIETY OF CAMPAIGNS TO SPARE ITS MEMBERSHIP FROM IMPRISONMENT."

demonstrations, or other seemingly mundane (and constitutionally protected) activities. Many of the party's early recruits had spent time in prison, either as juveniles or adults, and so imprisonment was already a familiar reality to many of them.[3]

In just two years, the Black Panther Party had grown from an Oakland-based group to an organization with chapters around the world. Its swift growth owed to many things, including the shifting political winds occasioned by the 1968 assassination of Martin Luther King Jr. and, seven months later, the election of Richard Nixon. However, perhaps the most immediate reason for the BPP's rapid rise owed to its skillful demands for the freedom of black political prisoners—including its own leadership. Between 1967 and 1972, the organization waged a variety of campaigns to spare its membership from imprisonment.

The first such case was in many respects the most dramatic: BPP co-founder Huey P. Newton was arrested on October 28, 1967, for the death of police officer John Frey. Newton and another officer were also wounded in the incident. Newton faced the death penalty if

convicted. Thus, the organization dedicated its resources to saving his life.

The "Free Huey" campaign preoccupied the Panthers and garnered a significant amount of media attention throughout 1968, helped by Newton's commitment to serving as a visible party leader by issuing decrees and giving interviews despite and even because of his incarceration. To celebrate his twenty-sixth birthday in February 1968 thousands of people rallied in Oakland and Los Angeles. In what would become a common occurrence in such defense efforts, the rallies brought together high-profile black activists, civil libertarians, and prominent actors.

It was perhaps the largest such effort since the Rosenberg case of the early 1950s. The campaign for Newton, equally emphasizing his innocence and the "system's" guilt, brought greater numbers of people to focus on exposing the cruelties of imprisonment. "Free Huey" became not just a demand bearing on a legal case but an extension of the Panthers' ten-point program for socialism and an end to white supremacy. Initially convicted of voluntary manslaughter in 1968,

Newton's conviction was overturned in 1970. In that time, dozens of new Panther chapters formed around the world and Newton became a household name.[4]

Much of the Free Huey campaign was organized by former prisoner turned author, journalist, and Black Panther minister of information Eldridge Cleaver. Cleaver had been in and out of prison since the age of twelve on charges that included burglary, drug possession, and assault with intent to kill, a 1957 charge that stemmed from a rape. Convicted of that offense, Cleaver became a leader of the Nation of Islam while at San Quentin and at Folsom prisons, but left the organization when Malcolm did. Inspired by Malcolm X, Cleaver became a writer while incarcerated. His literary potential helped earn his release in 1966, and resulted in the 1968 publication of a book of his prison writings, *Soul on Ice,* which became a bestseller. Cleaver fled the country to avoid returning to prison after a shootout with police. Other Black Power activists would embrace exile over the threat of prison, going to places such as Algeria, Cuba, France, and Tanzania.

The turn to defense campaigns, which

Black Panther Party co-founder and chairman Bobby Seale defined political prisoners in these terms: "To be a Revolutionary is to be an enemy of the state. To be arrested for this struggle is to be a political prisoner." James Baldwin visits Seale in the San Francisco County Jail, 1969. Baldwin was close to the BPP and spoke in the United States and in Europe on behalf of American political prisoners. © Stephen Shames.

became increasingly important as the FBI and local police sought to destroy the organization, brought the Panthers into ever larger coalitions with diverse groups of activists and civil libertarians. In Chicago, police bound and gagged Panther co-founder Bobby Seale in a courtroom when he insisted on having an attorney of his choosing. Shortly thereafter, Seale stood trial with Panther Ericka Huggins in New Haven on charges of having killed a member of the group. When the jury deadlocked in favor of acquittal, the judge dismissed the case. (Three others had already been convicted in the slaying.) In New York City, twenty-one Panthers were indicted on a series of specious charges in 1969. Even though a jury acquitted the group in under an hour in 1971, the two years it took to bring the case to trial decimated the organization. In fact, the case hastened the decline of the Black Panther Party as a global organization.

While public support flowed to the defendants in these and other cases, the Black Panther Party could not withstand the accelerated internecine battles already tearing it apart—tensions stoked by thick webs of government surveillance and infiltration. Some members elected to go underground, forming a loosely networked organization called the Black Liberation Army (BLA). Beginning

in 1971, BLA members carried out a series of robberies, attacks on police officers, and prison escapes over a ten-year period. Several members died in these efforts. Others became political prisoners. Forty-five years later, many of them remain in prison.

Other Black Power groups fared little better. Formed in the bustling Black Power metropolis of Detroit, for instance, the Republic of New Afrika had been attacked by police and the FBI in Detroit in 1969 and Jackson, Mississippi, in 1971. Eleven members were arrested in the latter raid, and they spent much of the 1970s appealing their case to the United Nations and other international entities. New Afrikan ideas, which hold that the transatlantic slave trade forged a new identity in need of redress, continue to hold sway in contemporary prison politics.

———

The defense campaign became increasingly important as the FBI and local police sought to destroy the BPP. Rallies to free all political prisoners mobilized large crowds. Oakland, 1968. © Stephen Shames.

THE PRISON REBELLION YEARS, 1968–1980

The success of the defense campaigns made it possible for people in prison to raise their own protests against dehumanizing conditions and racist violence. By the late 1960s, Black Power had moved into prison. These efforts led to some tangible changes in policy—for the better and the worse—as prisoners demanded adequate legal representation, medical care, and reading materials; an end to racist abuse by guards; and the right to organize.

But perhaps most significant was the ways in which these campaigns refashioned a conversation about prisons and political prisoners. Defense campaigns had focused largely on people arrested for their activism. They relied on a straightforward protest against

political repression: the government was criminalizing dissent and trying to do away with disruptive groups and individuals. That members of Richard Nixon's administration openly voiced such opinions made this argument appear almost self-evident to some.

However, as Black Power entered prison, the case became more complex. It was no longer a matter of asserting the innocence of the accused. After all, here were people who had already been convicted. Rather, Black Power activists in prison increasingly called into question the purpose of prison itself. To be sure, the presence of seasoned militants from the Black Panther Party (and later, the Black Liberation Army), the Nation of Islam, the Republic of New Afrika, the Revolutionary Action Movement, the Student Nonviolent Coordinating Committee, Us

DR. MUHAMMAD AHMAD (MAXWELL C. STANFORD JR.)
My Experience in the Black Power Movement

I co-founded the Revolutionary Action Movement (RAM) in the 1960s and the Afrikan People's Party in the 1970s. My memories of the period are of constant police and legal harassment. I first came under police harassment after the assassination of Malcolm X, when the Bureau of Secret Service, the political intelligence wing of the New York Police Department, was throwing bottles at my apartment at Ashland Place and a brother and I came out with rifles at about two or three o'clock in the morning. On another occasion I was subpoenaed by a federal grand jury. They questioned why I went to Cuba. I said it was because I wanted to study Cuban art.

I was subpoenaed by a federal grand jury for the so-called Statue of Liberty bomb plot and, in the middle of the grand jury, they said that they had changed the federal grand jury to study whether people would be indicted for un-American activities. I was the first to be investigated. I pleaded the Fifth Amendment so often they said that if I pleaded the Fifth any longer I would be incarcerated indefinitely. So the next time they asked me a question, I told them that on May 27, 1963, I was beaten unconscious by ten police officers and periodically had amnesia. On the morning that John Lewis was beaten in Selma, Alabama, I drafted a statement charging the grand jury with psychological genocide.

Organization, and others played a key role. But they merely accelerated dynamics that had already existed.

Throughout the 1960s and 1970s, black prisoners keenly followed world events. Many of them had been stopped, searched, beaten, or arrested by police on a number of occasions prior to their incarceration. Most of them were serving lengthy sentences for relatively minor crimes, and they welcomed the development of the civil rights and Black Power movements, as well as the anticolonial movements overseas. They were eager to apply the urgency of social change to their own austere conditions.

And so, prisoners formed study and self-defense groups. They taught each other how to read, using everything from *The Autobiography of Malcolm X* and *The Wretched of the Earth* (Frantz Fanon) to *Capital* (Karl

There were at least fifteen prison riots in 1968. The number increased until it reached an all-time high of forty-eight in 1972. Prisoners took over Attica prison in New York on September 9, 1971, and issued a series of demands that connected their conditions to war, racism, and poverty. Ten guards and twenty-nine prisoners were killed when the prison was retaken two days later. Associated Press.

———

Marx) and *The Prince* (Machiavelli). Many began to write letters, articles, and poetry for the first time. They learned self-defense in an effort to square off against white supremacist prisoners and racist guards. They authored petitions, appealed to the United Nations, published their own newspapers, and staged strikes and uprisings where other modes of protest failed to yield

The year 1965 was difficult. In May, *Life* magazine published an article titled, "The Plot to Get Whitey," which stated that I was the head of one thousand blood brothers who were planning urban guerilla warfare in the United States. I didn't have the money to sue *Life* magazine. My lawyer, Sam Siegel, said that the FBI would give the magazine all the information they had, so if there were any sort of truth to what had been published, it would be a difficult case to win in court.

In 1966 in New York, Queen Mother Audley Moore was having weekly rallies on Friday evenings to discuss the state of the Black Power movement. We asked Stokely Carmichael if we could develop a northern support wing of the Lowndes County Freedom Organization called the Black Panther Party that would advance the southern drive for the incorporation of elected officials on an independent political basis. Stokely approved, so we formed the New York Black Panther Party. The center was in Harlem

on 145th Street. But by this time, I had already been a target of the intelligence apparatus since 1964 or 1965. So, as we formed the Black Panther Party, I could be walking down 135th Street and a police helicopter would be flying over my head. I jaywalked two or three times and the helicopter would jaywalk with me; I would have to walk zigzag or duck through alleys to evade this helicopter. Brothers were telling me I was hot and I had to get out of the country, but I had nowhere to go and my passport had been taken.

There was always surveillance, but the repression hadn't really come yet. The first time Stokely spoke in New York, he came and left. The next time we were going to discuss strategy. We had to go into Mount Morris Park in twos. We sat up at the top and watched: as Stokely walked toward the park, there were police all over the place. The party was infiltrated from the start.

There was also interorganizational rivalry. Of course a lot of that was exacerbated by police

agencies. I operated in such a way that I would appear here, disappear there. I was told by some elder activists that I had about nine months to a year at the most. I was told that Hoover had called a secret joint session of Congress apparently to get some appropriation of funds and that I had been targeted. This was recorded in government documents, which I used to get a negotiated settlement from New York in 1973 or 1974. (I then decided to leave New York and to appear to cease my public organizing; I resettled in North Philadelphia.)

In a period of less than nine months in 1967, I was arrested about three or four times. Hoover came on TV and said I was the most dangerous man in America. This is when H. Rap Brown and Stokely were going around the country. Congress had passed a bill known as the Stokely Carmichael Bill and then they passed another bill to stop Rap. These bills made it a federal crime to advocate violent resistance while crossing state lines. I was

incarcerated several times and got bail.

Hoover was behind the Queens 17 case. It was called an assassination plot—a plot to assassinate Negro leaders. They even tried to include Bobby Kennedy. The district attorney promised Hoover that he could disrupt RAM. They did disrupt activities in Queens, but they didn't know about the existence of RAM in Brooklyn and Lower Manhattan. They also disrupted the study group we had in Harlem. I got out on bail, fought extradition, and got rearrested in Philadelphia for conspiracy to riot. After being held a month in Holmesburg prison, I was extradited to New York. When I was incarcerated in New York I couldn't make bail because I had ten cases in Philadelphia and ten charges in New York. Therefore, if I made bail in New York I would be extradited back to Philadelphia, my bail would be liquidated, and I would be re-incarcerated and sent back to New York.

I then picked up a case when three guards attacked me. I defended myself and was charged with assault. The next year, 1968, my bail was lowered. They changed the venue in order to find me guilty of assault and battery and to use that case to re-incarcerate me. I got out after Martin Luther King was assassinated—maybe two weeks later. The intelligence apparatus of the Muslims told me that I was being let out to be set up as a patsy for a nationwide sweep of all militants. RAM and the Black Guards had been told by the FBI to stay away from me once they were released because I was being let go for a big bust and anyone around me would be incarcerated. I figured that if I travelled around the country, I would be charged with conspiracy, so I had to bring the country to where I was. We maneuvered to have the Third Black Power Conference in Philadelphia, which about five thousand to seven thousand people attended.

Once in Chicago, two guys told me that Jeff Fort, the leader of the Blackstone Rangers, had held a press conference and said that I had given them dynamite the year before to blow up the presidential candidates at the National Democratic Convention in Chicago in 1968. Jeff Fort had first-degree murders on him. At that time I realized that no one had a defense against that kind of counterinsurgency or counterterrorism. Hoover had made me into a mythical devil figure. When I got arrested, they told me they were going to give me forty years and bury me.

There was a deliberate effort to destroy and annihilate most militant forces in the African American community at that time. My recollection is one of continuous jailing, continuous violation of my civil and human rights, and constant surveillance. Three times in my life I've ended up in pools of my own blood fighting for freedom, justice, and equality. If it weren't for the Black Power movement, fascism would probably have occurred much earlier.

In August 1971, San Quentin guards shot and killed George Jackson after he led a takeover of the solitary confinement unit. George Jackson's funeral in Oakland drew a massive crowd. © Stephen Shames.

change. They joined existing Black Power organizations—especially the Black Panther Party, which counted chapters from San Quentin, California, to Angola, Louisiana, and beyond—or formed their own. In these and related efforts, prisoners refused to be bound by the prison. They sought public contact through correspondence, publication, and by taking control of their own trials where possible.

These years of prison rebellion began as the years of urban rebellion were receding. There were at least fifteen prison riots in 1968. The number increased annually until it reached an all-time high of forty-eight in 1972. Most occurred in men's prisons, but several took place in women's institutions. Many of these uprisings, alongside an untold number of smaller disturbances and attacks on guards, raised explicitly political demands. In some of these rebellions—most famously the one at Attica (NY) in September 1971 but also Walpole (MA) from March to May 1973, Walla Walla (WA) between 1970 and 1974, and the Tombs city jail in New York—prisoners seized full or partial control of the institution. These uprisings were often multiracial affairs led by black prisoners.

George Jackson became a figurehead in the development of Black Power in prison. At eighteen years of age, he was sentenced to serve between one year and life in prison for a $70 gas station robbery in 1960. Increasingly politicized as the decade progressed, Jackson was one of several black prisoners challenging segregation within California prisons. In 1970, he and two other prisoners were accused of killing a Soledad prison guard in retaliation for the deaths of three black prisoners shot and killed by another guard. Supporters dubbed them the Soledad Brothers. Jackson was appointed field marshal of the Black Panther Party and tasked with recruiting more prisoners to the organization.

By the year's end, Jackson's letters had been compiled into a book, *Soledad Brother,*

> **" PRINT CULTURE BECAME THE BEST WAY PEOPLE IN PRISON HAD OF COMMUNICATING WITH EACH OTHER AND THE OUTSIDE WORLD. PRISONERS CREATED OR PARTICIPATED IN DOZENS OF MAGAZINES AND NEWSPAPERS IN THESE YEARS. "**

that gave voice to Black Power's prison organizing. "There are still some blacks here who consider themselves criminals—but not many. Believe me, my friend, with the time and incentive that these brothers have to read, study, and think, you will find no class or category more aware, more embittered, desperate, or dedicated to the ultimate remedy—revolution. The most dedicated, the best of our kind—you'll find them in the Folsoms, San Quentins, and Soledads. They live like there was no tomorrow. And for most of them there isn't."[5] In August 1971, San Quentin guards shot and killed Jackson after he led a bloody takeover of the solitary confinement unit in which he was held. Authorities allege it was an escape attempt but suspicions surrounding his death sparked international protest.

The Attica rebellion flowed directly out of a one-day fast that prisoners there held to commemorate Jackson's death. Prisoners took over the facility on September 9, 1971, and issued a series of demands that poignantly connected their conditions to war, racism, and poverty. They established an ad hoc commune in the yard for the length of the rebellion and assembled a negotiation team that included politicians, journalists, and social movement leaders. New York governor Nelson Rockefeller

refused to negotiate, however, and ordered state troopers to violently retake the prison on September 13. They did so with gas and guns, killing twenty-nine prisoners as well as ten guards who had been taken as hostages.

Several prisoners continued to fight for Black Power behind bars in the 1970s, often drawing explicit inspiration from Jackson. But as conditions grew more severe, there were fewer opportunities to organize. Print culture became the best way people in prison had of communicating with each other and the outside world. Prisoners created or participated in dozens of magazines and newspapers in these years. And black prisoners led rebellions in places such as Indiana and Alabama.

Some of the most successful Black Power prisoners were women. Perhaps the most famous was Jackson's close friend Angela Davis. Davis was a young philosophy professor, a prominent member of the Communist Party, and a leader of the Soledad Brothers Defense Committee. She was charged with supplying the guns that her bodyguard, Jackson's seventeen-year-old younger brother, Jonathan, used in an ill-fated attempt to free three black prisoners in August 1970. Jackson and two of the prisoners were killed in the attempt, along with a judge. Davis went underground but was arrested two months later. She spent sixteen months in pretrial detention, much of it in solitary confinement. During that time, she wrote several influential critiques of imprisonment and slavery. After a worldwide campaign demanded her freedom, she was acquitted in 1972.

Angela Davis's case was the most famous in a series of cases involving women activists. Some, such as Assata Shakur and Safiya Bukhari, came directly out of the Black Power movement. Shakur and Bukhari were both members of the Black Panther Party and charged with participating in the Black Liberation Army. Shakur was arrested and shot with her hands up on the New Jersey Turnpike in 1973. She was sentenced to life in prison for the death of a state trooper killed during her arrest, despite the fact that she had not fired a gun. She escaped from prison in 1979 and ultimately took up residence in Cuba, where she remains in exile. Bukhari was arrested in a Virginia grocery store in 1975 and sentenced to forty years for robbery. In poor health but denied medical care, Bukhari also escaped. Rearrested two months later, she pointed to the medical neglect as the cause for her escape. She received a needed hysterectomy but was placed in solitary confinement. Bukhari was paroled in 1983 and became a lifelong advocate for black political prisoners until her death in 2003.

Other prominent cases, however, did not involve famous activists. Perhaps the most unexpected example of black political prisoners in this time period came in the case of Joan Little. The twenty-year-old Little was serving seven to ten years in a North Carolina jail for robbery when she killed a sixty-two-year-old prison guard who had just sexually assaulted her. Little's case brought together an impressive coalition of Black Power activists, feminists, prison reform advocates, and others. In a time when some feminists were pursuing stronger criminal sanctions for gender violence, her case extended Black Power's critique of the criminal justice system to identify its inability to protect black women. Her acquittal in 1975 helped establish legal precedent for women's self-defense against physical and sexual abuse.[6]

TOP: *Black Panther Assata Shakur (Joanne Chesimard) was accused of being a member of the Black Liberation Army and was sentenced to life in prison for the death of a state trooper killed during her arrest on the New Jersey Turnpike in 1973. She escaped from prison in 1979 and lives in Cuba. 1977. AP Photo/File.*
MIDDLE: *George Jackson was a figurehead in the development of Black Power in prison, which called into question the purpose of prison itself. The author of* Soledad Brother *was field marshal of the Black Panther Party and tasked with recruiting prisoners to the organization. San Quentin, 1971. © Stephen Shames.*
BOTTOM: *Geronimo (Elmer) Pratt, also known as Geronimo ji-Jaga, was the minister of defense of the Black Panther Party. Convicted of kidnapping and murder, Pratt spent twenty-seven years in prison. His sentence was vacated in 1997. Los Angeles, 1971. AP Photo/File.*

FROM BLACK POWER TO MASS INCARCERATION

The spread of Black Power through and against American prisons terrified officials. Authorities moved to thwart the movement's growing success—first through imprisonment itself, and, when that failed, by using censorship and solitary confinement to make life in prison more isolating and challenging. Prison authorities moved to restrict prison libraries and writing programs, eliminate subversive prisoner publications, and make it harder for people in prison to work together or with people on the outside.

By 1980, black political prisoners garnered far less public support or attention. Black Power activists continued to be arrested and imprisoned, however, as poor urban black communities bore the brunt of the nation's growing wars on crime and drugs. Former Black Panther turned journalist Mumia Abu-Jamal was arrested for the death of a police officer in 1981. Supporters, pointing to a host of trial irregularities, claim that he was framed. Global support succeeded in getting Abu-Jamal off death row but has failed to release him from prison.

Other black political prisoners from that era—among them Herman Bell, Romaine Chip Fitzgerald, Jalil Muntaqim, Ed Poindexter, and members of the Philadelphia-based black naturalist MOVE organization—have been routinely denied parole, as politically appointed parole boards bow to the intense public pressure by police unions. Several former Black Panthers have died in prison, including Kuwasi Balagoon (1986), Merle Africa (1998), Albert Nuh Washington (2000), Teddy Jah Heath (2001), Bashir Hameed (2008), and Phil Africa (2015). Herman Wallace, one of the founders of the Angola Prison Black Panther chapter, who was kept in solitary confinement for almost forty years, was granted compassionate release three days before he died in October 2013.[7] A few black political prisoners—Marshal Eddie Conway, Sekou Kambui, and Sekou Odinga—were released in 2014. At least two others, Sundiata Acoli and Mutulu Shakur, have been promised release but remain incarcerated after more than forty and thirty years, respectively. Additionally, since 9/11, law enforcement has attempted to prosecute several aging black radicals for forty-year-old crimes with mixed results.

Beginning in the mid-1970s, the U.S. prison population began a meteoric rise that today has given this country the largest prison system in the world. Fifty years after the rise of the Black Power movement, several activists from that era—mostly veterans of the Black Panther Party—remain in prison. The prison population has grown more than 500 percent since 1980. The racial disparities of U.S. incarceration trump that of apartheid South Africa. Thirteen percent of the population as a whole, black people comprised almost 40 percent of the more than 2.2 million people incarcerated in American jails and prisons in 2012. The United States incarcerates more people and at a higher rate than anywhere on the planet; more people are being forced into prison for less cause, staying there longer, and being treated worse during and after their incarceration.[8]

Several veterans of the Black Power movement have formed organizations to counteract these disturbing trends. Safiya Bukhari helped found the Jericho Amnesty Movement to free U.S. political prisoners and remained tirelessly devoted to this cause until her death. Other former political prisoners—Ashanti Alston, Masai Ehosai, Herman Ferguson, and Kazi Toure—have been centrally involved in the Jericho movement. Angela Davis was part of the founding collective of Critical Resistance, a prison abolition organization, and remains a popular speaker on matters of race, justice, and punishment.

The Black Power movement challenged both the prison of American racism and the racism of American prisons. A half century later, the interrelationship between prisons, policing, and racism remains a central example of American inequality. The killing of black men, women, and children by police and vigilantes since 2012 alone—Trayvon Martin, Renisha McBride, John Crawford, Tamir Rice, Eric Garner, Ezell Ford, Mike Brown, Yvette Smith, Walter Scott, and literally dozens of others—has generated a new social movement under the slogan of #BlackLivesMatter. Activists have staged bold protests against these killings, taking

over highways and shutting down police stations in attempts to hold police accountable.

At the same time, prisons have once again become political battlegrounds. Between 2011 and 2013, prisoners in California staged three hunger strikes against long-term solitary confinement. The last and largest strike had thirty thousand participants. Smaller but sizable hunger and labor strikes by people in prison have also taken place in Georgia, North Carolina, Ohio, and elsewhere. Also in that time period, the controversial incarceration of several black women and transgender people for physically defending themselves against abuse have renewed conversations about racism, gender violence, and the failings of the criminal justice system.[9]

Formerly incarcerated people have also increased their activism and visibility. Organizations such as All of Us or None have noted the ways in which a criminal record has been used as the pretext for political disenfranchisement and social exclusion. On the fiftieth anniversary of the 1965 Selma to Montgomery march, a group of formerly

On October 13, 1970, after two months on the run, Angela Davis was arrested by the FBI in New York. Rallies to get her freedom were held all over the country and abroad. An all-white jury acquitted her in June 1972. New York, April 3, 1973. AP Photo.

incarcerated people marched "backwards," from Montgomery to Selma, to symbolically mark the ways in which imprisonment has justified backtracking on matters of racial justice. They carried a banner protesting the move "from the back of the bus to the front of the prison."

These twenty-first-century campaigns have often drawn explicitly on an earlier generation's efforts to free black political prisoners. The future remains uncertain, but one thing is clear: as long as the criminal justice system continues to be a barometer of injustice, the work of the Black Power movement against criminalization will continue.

Twenty artists affiliated with the Organization of Black American Culture (OBAC) created the Wall of Respect in 1967 on the South Side of Chicago. Additions were made in 1969. © Darryl Cowherd.

CHAPTER 5

The Black Arts Movement

James Smethurst

The Black Arts Movement (BAM) refers to a network of politically and formally radical black writers, visual artists, musicians, dancers, theater workers, and cultural organizers of the 1960s and 1970s. The term was coined by the poet, playwright, critic, and political activist Larry Neal after the usage of the term "Black Art" in the work of the poet, playwright, fiction writer, critic, and leading political activist Amiri Baraka (LeRoi Jones). The term also reflected the name of the Black Arts Repertory Theater and School (BARTS), which Neal helped found in Harlem alongside Baraka, poet and critic Askia Touré (Rolland Snellings), poet, playwright, fiction writer, and critic Sonia Sanchez, and other black artists, intellectuals, and political organizers.

As with any other artistic period or movement, it is not possible to date the BAM era precisely, but it is generally considered to have lasted from the mid-1960s to the mid- to late 1970s. It is also impossible to separate BAM from the Black Power movement. Black Power contained many sometimes conflicting strands, but one thing that connected virtually all of those strands was that black liberation and self-determination required

a raising, really a transformation, of black consciousness. Culture, in both its "high" and "popular" forms, was seen as both expressing and shaping consciousness. As a result, Black Power, by and large, was a formation that put a very strong emphasis on art and culture as key elements of political struggle. Similarly, BAM was a radical arts movement that, too, was aesthetically and ideologically diverse, but was connected by the belief that a major part of its work was promoting revolutionary social transformation. If, as a number of scholars have commented over the years, BAM was the cultural wing of Black Power, one might also say that Black Power was the political action wing of BAM. In truth, BAM and Black Power were not so much separate entities, but rather, as Larry Neal put it, "concepts" of, or ways of coming at, the black freedom movement. In that way of thinking, art was (or could be) political action just as those activities usually considered to be political were a sort of art.

THE ORIGINS AND GROWTH OF BAM

There were many streams of political and aesthetic thought and practice that flowed into BAM. However, the key influence on its growth was probably Malcolm X.

Larry Neal was education director of the Black Panther Party and a member of the Revolutionary Action Movement (RAM). Together with Askia Muhammad Touré and Amiri Baraka, he was a principal mover in the group that created the Black Arts Repertory Theatre School in Harlem in 1964. Neal, a poet and playwright, was a leading contributor of the BAM. In "The Black Arts Movement," he explained how the movement was the "aesthetic and spiritual sister of the Black Power concept." Photographs and Prints Division, Schomburg Center for Research in Black Culture, The New York Public Library.

———

Consciousness and culture were at the heart of Malcolm X's speeches and writings on the necessary transformation of "Negroes" into "Black people," a transformation attended by notions of nationhood and self-determination. Malcolm X took up the question of aesthetics and artistic production on the most basic as well as the most subtle levels, describing the work of his Organization of Afro-American Unity as a grassroots "cultural revolution":

Our cultural revolution must be the means of bringing us closer to our African brothers and sisters. It must begin in the community and be based on community participation. Afro-Americans will be free to create only when they can depend on the Afro-American community for support, and Afro-American artists must realize that they depend on the Afro-American community for inspiration.[1]

Malcolm X also provided a practical impetus to the founding of BAM when he called for the establishment of a black cultural center and school in Harlem:

We must work toward the establishment of a cultural center in Harlem, which will include people of all ages and will conduct workshops in all of the arts, such as film, creative writing, painting, theater, music, and the entire spectrum of Afro-American history.[2]

> ## " THERE WERE MANY STREAMS OF POLITICAL AND AESTHETIC THOUGHT AND PRACTICE THAT FLOWED INTO BAM. HOWEVER, THE KEY INFLUENCE ON ITS GROWTH WAS PROBABLY MALCOLM X. "

When Amiri Baraka left the downtown New York City bohemia of Greenwich Village and the Lower East Side to join with other black artists, intellectuals, and activists in founding BARTS in Harlem after the murder of Malcolm X in 1965, it was with the sense of answering this call for a cultural center in Harlem that would be part of a larger struggle for black liberation. Baraka made this connection quite explicit when he sent a letter to many of the black artists, writers, theater workers, musicians, and intellectuals of New York City, calling on them to join in the BARTS project and continue Malcolm X's work. It was in this spirit that Baraka and other radical black artists and intellectuals, including Sanchez, Barbara Ann Teer, Touré, Neal, Sun Ra, and Abbey Lincoln, joined in the activities of the first major black cultural institution to use the term "Black Arts" in its title, giving shape to the idea of a coherent movement working toward a more or less common goal.

Another major inspiration for BAM was the rise of "new jazz" (or the "new thing" or "free jazz") at the end of the 1950s and the beginning of the 1960s, which signaled a break with "western" popular and "art" music. While in some respects one could see this jazz as a revival of the experimental or radical aesthetic impulse of bebop, in many respects it also sounded a new internationalist aesthetic, a sort of "Bandung" (after the landmark 1955 conference of new African and Asian nations and independence movements in Bandung, Indonesia) aesthetic. John

Coltrane was the most important innovator in this mode, becoming a popular figure in BAM poetry. One might see Coltrane as the epitome of a sort of Bandung jazz. He directly incorporated elements and approaches of Latin American, Caribbean, and African music to his melodies, harmonies, and rhythms, as jazz musicians had been doing for some time, but also deeply engaged Asian, especially South Asian musical influences. Other leading older new jazz figures included pianist Cecil Taylor, alto saxophonist Ornette Coleman, tenor saxophonist Albert Ayler, multi-reed player Eric Dolphy, and pianist, composer, and big-band leader Sun Ra. These musicians were innovative, yet also affirmed—often prominently—their connection to black musical tradition. This not only presented a model of approaching African American (and African and African diasporic) cultural and social heritage and approaching black audiences for black artists in other genres and media, but also a crucial sense that black people were on the cutting edge of artistic creation, both nationally and internationally. As Baraka noted, "We knew the music was hip and new and out beyond anything anyone downtown was doing, in music, painting, poetry, dance. . . . And we felt, I know I did, that we were linked to that music that Trane and Ornette and C.T., Shepp and Dolphy and the others, were making, so the old white arrogance and elitism of Europe as Center Art was stupid on its face."[3]

Another important factor in the growth of BAM was the eruption of massive urban

uprisings across the country, beginning with New York, Jacksonville, and a number of smaller New Jersey cities in 1964 and dramatically escalating with Watts in 1965, Cleveland in 1966, and Detroit and Newark in 1967. One aspect of the influence of these uprisings was ideological. These rebellions were generally touched off by some act of police violence or harassment, but were also the product of resentment over discrimination in housing, employment, education,

policing, and, really, practically every aspect of urban life. While the growing number of radical black political and cultural organizations of various stripes had theorized, organized, and agitated for black rebellion, these urban uprisings far exceeded the expectations of all but the most optimistic black revolutionaries. They created an environment in which revolution, both domestically and internationally, seemed realistically imminent and they made radical cultural and political

> **" WHAT BARTS DID ... WAS TO PROVIDE BOTH A MODEL OF WHAT A BLACK REVOLUTIONARY ARTS INSTITUTION MIGHT BE AND A CALL FOR A MORE FOCUSED AND UNITED RADICAL BLACK CULTURAL MOVEMENT. "**

Artists of the BAM. Sitting from left: poet Nikki Giovanni and Evelyn Neal. Standing from left: designer Bob Rogers, writer Ishmael Reed, poet Jayne Cortez, Léon-Gontran Damas, who co-founded the Négritude movement, painter Romare Bearden, and playwright Larry Neal. The photo was taken by sculptor Mel Edwards. New York, 1969. © Melvin Edwards. Photographs and Prints Division, Schomburg Center for Research in Black Culture, The New York Public Library.

projects, institutions, and actions seem practical not only to radicals, but to many people hitherto outside black radical circles.

Part of the impact of the plausibility of mass social rebellion outside radical circles, including among liberal, centrist, and even conservative white political and economic leaders, was that large amounts of money and other resources were made available for public arts and educational initiatives, especially within the black community, often with

a quite radical character. BARTS, for example, was financed with public money under the Harlem Youth Opportunities Unlimited-Associated Community Teams (or HARYOU-ACT), significantly through the efforts of Harlem congressperson Adam Clayton Powell Jr., who argued for the money as part of a campaign to prevent more uprisings after 1964. This new stream of financing for public art, first in the black community—unthinkable even a couple of years before—points to the contradictory character of the time. On one hand, fear of black rebellion and even revolution, especially in conjunction with international liberation movements during the Cold War, helped channel a range of resources into black communities (and other communities) doing much to open up a public cultural sector. On the other hand, the same fear also stimulated the further growth of a repressive state apparatus already largely in place from the Cold War, perhaps most infamously the FBI's Counterintelligence Program (COINTEL-PRO), which sought to undermine, redirect, and eliminate BAM initiatives in many places.

Of course, BARTS was not the first radical grassroots black cultural institution or organization of the 1960s. The decade had seen a steady rise in such institutions and organizations under the influence of the civil rights movement; the increasing impact of Malcolm X, Elijah Muhammad, and the Nation of Islam; the nonaligned and independence movements of the nations and peoples formerly and currently under colonial and neocolonial rule; and important pockets of

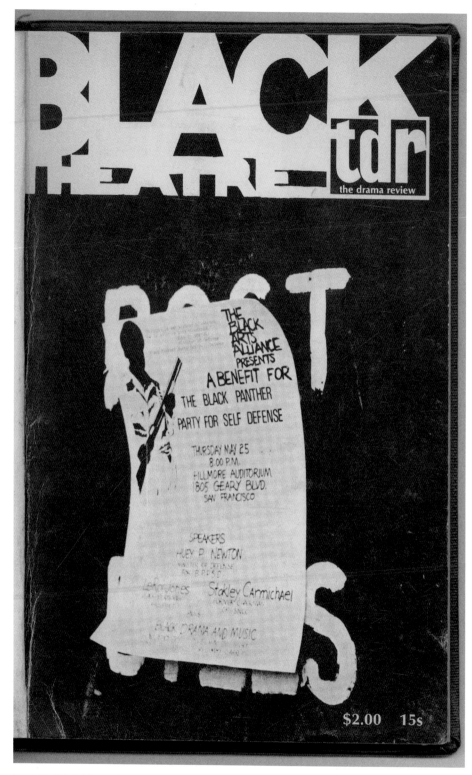

Larry Neal, LeRoi Jones, Jimmy Garrett, Sonia Sanchez, Marvin X, Ed Bullins, Bill Gunn, and John O'Neal con-
tributed articles to the Drama Review's *special issue on black theater. The flyer on the cover announced a benefit*
for the Black Panther Party. Summer 1968. Jean Blackwell Hutson Research and Reference Division, Schomburg
Center for Research in Black Culture, The New York Public Library.

Old Left (especially Communist Party and Socialist Workers Party) and Garveyite (and other forms of black nationalist) influence. For example, the emergence of quite a few radical black journals that would be important to the rise of BAM, such as *Liberator* (1961), *Umbra* (1961), *Freedomways* (1961), *Negro Digest* (1961), and *SoulBook* (1964), antedated Malcolm X's assassination and the founding of BARTS. Various proto-BAM workshops, theaters, galleries, museums, publishers, and so on, such as the Umbra Poets Workshop (New York City), On Guard for Freedom (New York City), the Watts Repertory Theatre (Los Angeles), the Ebony Museum (later the DuSable Museum, Chicago), Broadside Press (Detroit), and the Free Southern Theater (Tougaloo, Mississippi and then New Orleans), also predated or arose at more or less the same time as BARTS.

What BARTS did, however, was to provide both a model of what a black revolutionary arts institution might be and a call for a more focused and united radical black cultural movement. This it did with a sense of its mission to continue, flesh out, and extend Malcolm X's thoughts on culture as a key component of a black liberation movement that sought to engage the broad population of African Americans in the communities where they lived.

In this, BARTS was simultaneously a failure and a success. It was a failure in the sense that it was short lived, lasting less than a year. This was due largely to conflicts and contradictions caused by unstable partici- pants, culminating in a series of violent or near-violent episodes, including the shoot- ing of Larry Neal in 1965. However, it was a success in that it fostered the performance of plays, poetry, and concerts, both in the BARTS building and in the streets and other public spaces, reaching thousands. And, again, in part because of the national repu- tation of Amiri Baraka following the success of his 1964 play Dutchman and because of a lingering sense of Harlem as the most important center of black art and politics in the United States (and perhaps the world), BARTS served as an inspiration for the cre- ation of like institutions (or the revolutionary recasting of existing institutions) elsewhere.

Even BARTS's collapse stimulated the growth of BAM across the nation. Following the organization's implosion, BARTS activists began to leave New York: Amiri Baraka back to his hometown of Newark, New Jersey (and then to San Francisco and back to New- ark), Sonia Sanchez to San Francisco, and Askia Touré to San Francisco. These former BARTS collaborators joined local black artists in starting new BAM institutions and groups, further spreading the movement. The migration of Sanchez, Baraka, and Touré to the West Coast to help found the first black studies program at San Francisco State also allowed them to join artists already in the Bay Area, such as playwright Ed Bullins, poet and playwright Marvin X, playwright Jimmy Garrett, poet and publisher Joe Goncalves, and poet and teacher Sarah Webster Fabio. These new collaborations served to build or strengthen the BAM infrastructure, including Black Arts West, the Black House, the *Journal of Black Poetry,* and the Black Communica- tions Project. However, the Bay Area was not immune to the conflicts that had attended BARTS. Stoked particularly by the Black Panthers under the leadership of Eldridge Cleaver, the Bay Area Black Power and Black Arts movements suffered a variety of disrup- tions and internal conflicts, leading quite a few black artists and activists, including San- chez, Baraka, Touré, Bullins, and Marvin X (for a time), to leave, contributing to the growth of BAM and black studies elsewhere.

In short, a number of factors made BAM possible as the nationally (and internation- ally) successful movement that it was: the influence of the more militant, direct-action wing of the civil rights movement, the non-aligned movement, and the independence movements of Africa, Asia, and Latin America; some diminishment of the antiradical repression of the domestic Cold War; the words, actions, and symbolic figure of Malcolm X (as well as those of Elijah Muhammad and the Nation of Islam more generally); and the new jazz avant-garde. Such elements promoted the growth of new radical black political and cultural institutions and organizations all across the country in the early 1960s, often within or growing out of spaces of the Old Left and various strains of older black nationalism, especially the Garvey movement. The eruption of rebellions in ghettos across the country promoted a sense of revolutionary possibility while shaking loose financial support for new cultural initiatives. The rise of the nationally prominent BARTS, a network of journals and presses (especially Broadside Press), and a series of high-profile political and cultural conferences that circulated radical black art and political thought across the United States (and beyond) began to give the various new local institutions, organizations, and artists an increased sense of being part of a national movement.

BAM AESTHETICS AND PRACTICE

It is not really possible to speak of a unified BAM aesthetic or artistic practice any more than it is possible to describe a single Black Power ideology or political approach. In many respects, BAM was more of a conversation or debate about common political and cultural concerns rather than a monolithic movement. In part, the diversity of aesthetics and practice was a function of the movement's success in reaching every city, town, campus, and so on, where there were any appreciable number of black people. Virtually any such place had a black bookstore, theater, poetry workshop, newspaper or magazine, gallery, visual arts program, neighborhood cultural center, and so on—most of the larger cities and campuses had all of these things. One obvious fact is that different places are different, with varied histories, demographics, and cultural and political traditions and experiences. In other words, New Orleans is not Detroit; San Francisco is not New York; Boston is not Houston; East St. Louis is not Atlanta; Los Angeles is not Philadelphia; Chicago is not Newark. What worked and made sense to people in one place was not necessarily practical in another, at least not without some translation.

Having said that, it is possible to make some generalization about BAM aesthetics and artistic practice. There was an almost universally shared sense that black people were, in fact, a people or a nation with the right to determine their own destiny politically, socially, culturally, and spiritually. How this would work on the ground was a matter of some debate, ranging from the establishment of a sovereign black state to what might be thought of as black-run city-states or communities within a larger polity. While there was considerable argument as to whether one worked with white radicals and liberals (at least, in theory, since virtually all BAM and Black Power activists worked with white radicals and liberals on a practical level, either occasionally or regularly), there was wide agreement that the racist political, social, and economic structure oppressed and exploited black people (and other people of color) and was in need of radical change, if not complete destruction. There was a general sense that in order for the black nation to advance, to successfully make its own destiny, a change in consciousness on the part of African Americans was necessary. This transformation would have to counter the psychological

W.E.B. Du Bois, Stokely Carmichael, Muhammad Ali, Malcolm X, Nina Simone, Amiri Baraka, John Coltrane, Thelonius Monk, Max Roach, H. Rap Brown, Charlie Parker, Wilt Chamberlain, and James Baldwin were some of the people honored on Chicago's Wall of Respect, which was destroyed by fire in 1971. © Darryl Cowherd.

brainwashing imposed on black people through, notably, mainstream popular and "high" culture, education, law, policing and incarceration, as well as determine what the content of the new blackness would be and how it would relate to black tradition. Again, as discerned by Malcolm X, art and culture were seen as key elements in that transformation of consciousness.

Consequently, there came to be a considerable interest in establishing, or at least theorizing, a black aesthetic by which black art and culture could be evaluated and taught and through which new art could be created in a manner that promoted black self-determination. The idea was that the sorts of aesthetic notions of beauty, value, truth, and so forth, that had been canonized in the past (and were generally taught in the present educational system) were not only parochial white notions masquerading as universal, but were part of a system created for, among other things, political domination of black people. Once more, this discussion of black aesthetics and a usable black artistic past were just that, a discussion or debate, not a papal decree from on

high. There was a tendency, perhaps most clearly exemplified by the neo-Africanist thought of Maulana Karenga's Kawaida-ism, that argued that the blues, R & B, and older black popular culture generally were products of a past of slavery, Jim Crow, and black self-hatred or defeatism and, as such, needed to be abandoned in favor of a new liberated culture based in idealized versions of a precolonial African past. Others theorized a continuum of black culture reaching back to Africa and moving forward through black popular music and culture to the new jazz avant-garde—all a necessary part of the emerging liberated black nation. Perhaps the most famous of these was Amiri Baraka with his concept of the "Changing Same" (despite the heavy influence of Karenga on Baraka during much of the BAM era). Still others, particularly the cultural activists of BLKARTSOUTH in New Orleans, while agreeing that some codified system of black aesthetic judgment might be useful sometime in the future, felt that it was much too soon to attempt to impose such a system. They felt that it would be much better for the new black artists to create a large body of work over a period of time and then draw some conclusions about principles of evaluation and practice from that body. Anything else would be arbitrary, limiting or deforming the achievements of the new movement, especially given its geographical and ideological diversity.

However, certain generalizations can be made about the BAM approach to artistic practice and audience—with the caveat that there were some important exceptions. It is crucial to remember that BAM was in almost every regional and local iteration a revolutionary movement that sought to radically change the world, particularly the United States, even if there was not agreement on exactly how and in what direction the world would be changed. That change would not happen unless the masses of black people were engaged. Consequently, BAM was an avant-garde or vanguard arts movement that sought to reach a popular audience rather than a small, hip coterie. There was a considerable emphasis on performance, especially in poetry, theater, dance, and music. These performances took place in almost every space where black people gathered: housing project courtyards and community rooms, street corners, bars, parks, schools, churches, union halls, theaters, community arts and cultural centers, local museums, political rallies, and conventions. Even the visual arts often took on a performative aspect. For example, when the Organization of Black American Culture (OBAC) Visual Arts Workshop created the multimedia mural *Wall of Respect* in Chicago in 1967, a mural that was crucial to the growth of the public mural movement of the 1960s and 1970s, crowds of people watched the artists work as other sorts of artists, such as musicians, theater workers, and poets performed too.

The multimedia and multigeneric creation of the *Wall of Respect* also raises another aspect of BAM aesthetics and poetics. While one can talk of BAM painting, poetry, drama, dance, photography, music, or fiction, in point of fact it was often hard to make such distinctions of genre and media in actual practice since a typical BAM performance or text often blurred or erased such boundaries. For example, if one went to a "concert" of Sun Ra and his Arkestra and heard music

that included neo-African tunes, early New Orleans jazz, swing, bebop, R & B vocal music, and avant-garde jazz; saw the theater of the band in their "space" costumes; listened to Sun Ra's poetry; watched dancers (such as Vertamae Grosvenor) perform; and witnessed the light show of Sun Ra's light organ and other sorts of projects, how would one classify it? Even texts could be ambiguous, such as Sonia Sanchez's "On Seeing Pharaoh Sanders Blow" or "a/coltrane/poem." Not only did those texts often reference music, but the use of space and lineation on the page suggested the actual performance of music, providing a sort of score for reading the poem. Even at major (and less prominent) political events, conventions, and meetings, the lines between speech and artistic performance blurred. For example, when Amiri Baraka ended his main speech to the founding convention of the Congress of African People in 1970 with the poem "It's Nation Time," he did not set off the poem from the rest of his speech; it was all of a piece.

THE END OF BAM AND ITS LEGACIES

As with its beginning, it is as difficult to firmly mark the ending of BAM. Certainly by the middle of the 1970s internal ideological struggles between Marxists and anti-Marxist nationalists took a toll on many Black Power and Black Arts organizations and institutions. To some degree the success of Black Power and BAM also caused a certain amount of conflict as more centrist black political and cultural activists pulled away from the more revolutionary strains of those movements, finding new opportunities within the system that BAM and Black Power opened up. After the election of Ronald Reagan in 1980, a long process of political policing of and cuts to public arts programs and resources brought the already declining BAM to an end.

However, even though many major BAM institutions and organizations collapsed, others survived and flourished, such as the ETA Theater, Third World Press, and OBAC in Chicago; the National Black Theatre and the New Federal Theater in New York; the National Center of Afro-American Artists and its museum in Boston; and the African

American Museum in Philadelphia. BAM figures, such as Amiri and Amina Baraka in Newark, Sonia Sanchez in Philadelphia, Haki Madhubuti in Chicago, Eugene Redmond in St. Louis/East St. Louis, and Tom Dent in New Orleans remained central cultural and political figures locally as well as nationally even after the decline of BAM, inspiring the creation of new black art and education institutions, especially with the rise of black politicians to elective office. For example, Atlanta, particularly after the election of Maynard Jackson in 1973 and his decision to be the "culture mayor," was and still is a premier site of the institutionalization and continuing influence of BAM. All black artists (indeed, all artists and audiences for art in the United States) who came after BAM have had to grapple with its legacy. Perhaps ironically, BAM was a radical nationalist movement that placed black artists at the center of art in the United States. For example, it is impossible to understand both the development of Toni Morrison's fiction and the place it has in the literature of the United States without taking account of BAM.

BAM did much to change how all people in the United States understand what art is, what it is for, and how one receives it. Before BAM, the notion that a work could be serious, even radical, in form and content, was not widely accepted. Now such an understanding of popular culture is standard. This change can be clearly seen in hip-hop, where even artists not known as "conscious" regularly reach many millions, perhaps billions, of people with politically and formally radical work, such as Kanye West with "New Slave" and Lil Wayne with "God Bless America." Hip-hop also exemplifies the mixture of genres and media, combining music (past and present), poetry, dance, theater, and film/video in a radically hybrid form that can be found in other areas of popular and "high" culture. This breakdown of boundaries of genre, media, and audience has made it possible for artists such as Pearl Cleage and Sister Souljah to mix popular fiction genres (including urban romance, street lit, urban fantasy, science fiction, and detective) with black nationalist ideology and reach mass black audiences largely outside of mainstream channels of publicity, distribution, and reviewing.

BAM also changed how Americans felt that art should be circulated. The BAM imperatives of art for, by, and of black people in the communities in which they lived (as opposed to in elite museums, theaters, concert halls, for example, in which they often felt unwelcome), opened up the cultural landscape for publicly funded art and arts institutions aimed at grassroots communities. One might say that BAM practically invented or reinvented the public sector of the arts in a way that had not been seen since the New Deal, both on the local and state levels as well as in national institutions that reached millions of Americans generally, such as the Public Broadcasting System and National Public Radio, both founded in the late 1960s. In short, BAM reached millions of people through its journals, presses, theaters, murals, festivals, television shows such as *Soul!* and *Like It Is,* during the 1960s and 1970s, but it also left a lasting imprint on our sense of what art is, what it can do, and who it is for that remains with us to this day.

———

Askia Muhammad Touré, a leading poet, often considered the most influential poet-professor in the movement, was involved in most of the media (books, periodicals, and publishing company) through which the Black Arts Movement disseminated its creations. Black Poetry Festival at the Countee Cullen Branch of the New York Public Library, 1970. Art and Artifact Division, Schomburg Center for Research in Black Culture, The New York Public Library.

Black Poetry Festival

ASKIA MUHAMMAD TOURÉ

reading from his own works

Askia Muhammad Toure', poet-essayist, lecturer.
Editor-at-Large for the Journal of Black Poetry,
Contributing Editor for Black Theater magazine.
Widely published: work has appeared in Negro Digest
(now Black World), Freedomways, Black Dialogue,
Soulbook, Black Theater, and other publications.

Featured in the anthologies:
    Black Fire -- LeRoi Jones, Larry Neal
    Black Art -- Ahmed Alhamisi, Kofi Wangara
    Black Nationalism in America -- John Bracey,
            August Meier, Elliott Rudwick.

Has recently published a volume of poetry, JuJu
produced by Third World Press of Chicago, Illinois.
Editor of the Pan African edition of the Journal
of Black Poetry (Spring/Summer, 1970) issued
this month.

Wednesday   June 24, 1970   8:00 P.M.

COUNTEE CULLEN BRANCH
The New York Public Library
104 West 136th Street

ADMISSION FREE

The Australian Black Panther Party was formed by Denis Walker in 1971. A year earlier, a delegation of Aborigines had participated in the Congress of African People meeting in Atlanta. Like the U.S. BPP, the Australian Panthers advocated armed self-defense. They organized political education classes, demanded land restitution, education, better housing, justice, an end to police brutality, and the "overthrow of the system." Corbis.

CHAPTER 6

International Dimensions of the Black Power Movement

Brenda Gayle Plummer

Black Power in the United States is often understood as having followed on the heels of the nonviolent civil disobedience campaigns in the South. According to that narrative, disappointments and disillusion with the pace of change and continued violent opposition to the freedom movement spurred interest in left-wing radicalism and Islam. We now know, however, that Black Power was in dialogue with civil rights, occupying the same time frame, and providing alternative ways of addressing the problems of injustice and inequality. It has also become increasingly clear that Black Power was a global phenomenon.

While the history of black insurgency in individual countries can be addressed without referring to the world as a whole, casting our net wider reveals a drama of transnational efforts to combat racism and imperialism. In the Caribbean, recognition that independence came short of fulfilling the hopes of the region's people contributed to the emergence of Black Power insurgencies there. The Caribbean is often marginalized in the American imagination, but just as U.S. history cannot be understood without grasping the African American role in it, African

American history is deeply inflected by its connections to Caribbean events, personalities, and aspirations. Broad-based discontent with metropolitan powers and home governments alike prompted similar responses. Black Power cannot be situated within a single country but emerged across the diaspora of Africa-descended peoples.

Some scholars trace Black Power back to the early 1900s and link it to both domestic and international movements as part of a global black radical tradition.[1] They claim that Black Power activists of the 1960s and 1970s rejoined a long history of insurgency, an all-inclusive struggle with roots in the fight against slavery, that brought them fresh perspectives on the meaning of freedom and how to achieve it. The U.S. civil rights movement had framed black freedom within the boundaries of American citizenship, but Black Power internationalists perceived American claims to universalism as part of the problem that black people faced.

The aim of racial advancement characterized many of the political initiatives that people of African descent undertook in the twentieth century. Garveyite plans to establish Liberian cooperatives in the 1920s, for example, and defend Ethiopia's sovereignty against Italian conquest a decade later, formed part of this effort. Self-help was a vital component of what contemporaries called racial uplift. When self-help entered the stream of ideas that are grouped together as Black Power, it strongly rejected white leadership and its accompaniments: accommodationism, gradualism, and compromise. Black Power advocates expressed skepticism about nonviolent civil disobedience and moral suasion. Unyielding

---

Black Power activists supported the Cuban Revolution. Assata Shakur, Eldridge Cleaver, Angela Davis, Huey Newton, Stokely Carmichael, and Robert Williams visited Cuba or went into exile there. The relationship between black activists and Cuba had started years before. Robert Williams (seated center), Amira Baraka (to his right), and John Henrik Clarke (standing between them) with Cuban intellectuals in Havana in July 1960 during a tour of the Fair Play for Cuba Committee. Photographs and Prints Division, Schomburg Center for Research in Black Culture, The New York Public Library.

opposition from American segregationists and white settlers in southern Africa alike seemed to demonstrate the limitations of those techniques.

Black Power movements also influenced the way that Europeans and North American whites interpreted the issues that they also confronted as subjects of empire. Studies of their interactions with blacks, such as the celebrity expatriates who left the Jim Crow United States or stagnating colonies for comparatively tolerant metropoles, too often view these relationships as one-way exchanges. As Yohuru Williams wrote of African Americans abroad, their engagements are often viewed as "the product of foreign influences that extended from Marcus Garvey and Frantz Fanon to Che Guevara and Mao Tse-tung. Such images create the impression

that African Americans were greatly influenced by foreign contacts with little impact or contribution of their own."[2] Closer examination, however, yields insights into more complex patterns of communication.

Black Power revolt took place in the United States, Canada, and the Caribbean at nearly the same time with a similar vocabulary of protest. This suggests that we can fruitfully examine it as an international phenomenon and not always as confined to a specific place. Looking at Black Power through the lens of a moral geography leads us to a fresh look at how it operated in the course of the twentieth century. Michael J. Shapiro used the term "moral geography" to explain how "cultural and political struggles" that "do not appear on the map" nevertheless dispute commonplace understandings about how space is organized

Black Power militants interpreted the leading world issues through the lens of Cold War competition and stressed how racism and imperialism helped maintain unjust regimes. They were ideologically close to Socialist regimes in Tanzania, Guinea, Vietnam, Cuba, Algeria, and North Korea. Stokely Carmichael visits Troung Ching, chairman of the Permanent Committee of the Vietnam Democratic Republic National Assembly in Hanoi, 1967. © Bettmann/Corbis.

KATHLEEN NEAL CLEAVER

Art and Revolution[1]

1969. Algiers. The spectacular panorama of the first Pan-African Cultural Festival transformed the North African capital basking in the July sun. Musicians, dancers, horsemen, poets and painters, writers, filmmakers, scholars, and political leaders filled the city's hotels. Southern African freedom fighters and veteran guerillas from Angola, Mozambique, and Guinea-Bissau at war with the Portuguese joined the colorful delegations arriving from all over the vast continent. Algeria, chosen by the Organization of African Unity to host the festival, insisted that liberation from colonial rule was as central to African unity as music. President Houari Boumediene, a military leader during their war for independence from France, said at the opening ceremony that "culture is a weapon in our struggle for liberation."[2] His words applied equally to the effervescent affirmation of black culture we were experiencing in the U.S. where the black power movement fueled popular rejection of all varieties of racist control. African, Arab, European, and American visitors mingled with the invited artists and revolutionaries, including a delegation of Black Panthers, whom I was there to welcome. I'd just left my comrades that May in California, having barely escaped the dragnet pulling our leaders into prisons across the country.

I'd met Eldridge Cleaver, the

and reveal the underlying tensions behind the placid façade of conventional cartography.[3] How African Americans and others in the broader North American diaspora framed their practices drew considerable global interest and provided an inventory of symbols and practices used in other places. Black Power activism erased national boundaries as its strategies and tactics proved adaptable in a variety of circumstances.

The preacher and activist Malcolm X is a recognized progenitor of Black Power. As a Muslim, Malcolm's moral geography was pointed toward the Middle East and Africa. He inherited the Nation of Islam's stern critique of American racism and its awareness of international politics. As a minister of that organization in New York City, he famously frequented the UN delegates' lounge. There he cultivated Afro-Asian representatives and honed his understanding of world affairs. After Malcolm left the Nation of Islam, his internationalism grew stronger as a result of his religious and political travels. He sought to make the African American freedom movement part of a global thrust for colonial freedom and racial equality by appealing to the Organization of African Unity, the predecessor of today's African Union.[4]

Malcolm X did not live long enough to make his approach operational. The Student Nonviolent Coordinating Committee (SNCC), however, offers an example of how a civil rights organization came to identify itself with a mission that exceeded the territorial

information minister of the Black Panther Party, at a student conference on black liberation held in Nashville over the Easter weekend of 1967. We fell in love and by Christmas we were married. In late November 1968, Eldridge fled imprisonment in the wake of a gun battle between Black Panthers and Oakland police, and by the time I set out to join him I was seven months pregnant. Determined to be with my husband when our first child was born, I headed off for Havana, but discovered en route that the place we would meet was Algiers instead. Half a year after his clandestine departure from the United States, Eldridge Cleaver, celebrated author of *Soul on Ice* and fugitive revolutionary, was enthusiastically welcomed to Algiers on the eve of the Pan-African Cultural Festival.

On July 17, every seat inside la Mutualité, the auditorium where his press conference took place, was filled. Students, revolutionaries, Arabs, Europeans, Africans, and Black Americans all applauded Eldridge's arrival, acknowledging his presence in Algiers as a symbolic triumph over America's racist power. I felt electricity surge through the crowd when I walked onto the stage with Eldridge and his interpreter who translated his words into French. The charisma and authority in his voice, added to his imposing physical presence, brought an unexpected element into the excitement generated by the upcoming festival. Being in Africa, for him and the entire movement he represented, held deep significance for our fight for black liberation within America.

The Black Panther Party admired and studied Africa's struggles against colonialism, especially the Mau Mau rebellion in Kenya, Kwame Nkrumah's rise to power in Ghana, and the Algerian victory over French imperialism, which were catalysts to our battle for self-determination and civil rights. When the powerful film *The Battle of Algiers* was shown in the U.S., black revolutionaries identified strongly with the urban guerrillas fighting for national liberation who are the central figures of the drama. Even more pervasive was the transformative impact of the book *The Wretched of the Earth*, the seminal work of the French-trained Caribbean psychiatrist Frantz Fanon. His revolutionary analysis of the Algerian war, to which he ultimately dedicated his life, revealed so many parallels between the experience of colonial domination in Algeria and the racial oppression blacks had suffered for centuries in America that it made his work the essential text of the black liberation movement. Thus, visiting Algiers became almost a kind of pilgrimage for black revolutionaries in 1969.

The opening ceremony at the cultural festival coincided with the worldwide broadcast

Black Power activists opposed the war in Vietnam and found support among African American soldiers deployed there. U.S. Marine artillerymen at the Con Thien base supporting Black Power during the Vietnam War, 1968. AP Photo/Johner.

of dramatic images from the U.S. Apollo mission showing two men covered by silvery space suits plant an American flag on the moon. Journalists covering the first Pan-African Cultural Festival drawn to Eldridge Cleaver were filled with questions about this technological feat. Cleaver replied to the *New York Times* reporter, "I don't see what benefit mankind will have from two astronauts landing on the moon while people are being murdered in Vietnam and suffering from hunger even in the United States."[3] His sentiments resonated among many, particularly the contingent of Afro American artists and writers gathered in

Algiers, which included jazz musician Nina Simone, playwright Ed Bullins, and the poet Don Lee, later known as Haki Madhubuti. Black revolutionary leader Stokely Carmichael, formerly chairman of the radical Student Nonviolent Coordinating Committee, was also present; he was at the festival accompanying his wife, the exiled South African singer Miriam Makeba, who was a featured performer. By 1969 our artists and revolutionaries all drew strength from the momentum of the mass movement for black freedom that was accelerating daily, and connecting our cultural and political expressions at the deepest levels.

The festival provided the *Black Panther* delegation a ground floor commercial space with sparkling plate glass windows in the center of town to host an exhibit. We named it the Afro-American Information Center, where lively crowds of young Algerians clustered on the sidewalk to stare from the moment our artist Emory Douglas taped the first poster in the window. That was the large black-and-white poster boundaries of the United States. In December 1963 the State Department arranged a visit to Georgia by the Kenyan minister for foreign affairs Oginga Odinga. He was put up at an Atlanta hotel where he met with appreciative SNCC volunteers who knew him as a candid spokesperson for his country's independence and a forthright critic of racial discrimination. Atlanta's experiment with integration was limited, however. The SNCC representatives took Odinga to a nearby restaurant that refused to serve blacks. The episode ended with SNCC workers in jail and Odinga fully aware of the challenges the U.S. civil rights movement faced.

By this time SNCC had generated a following overseas, especially among students. Praise and testaments of solidarity arrived in SNCC's mailbox from Canada, the Netherlands, South Africa, and points beyond.

Messages of support encouraged the organization to seek out an audience beyond the borders of the United States. Its growing global outlook also derived from the international travel of some of its members, who as students or aid workers had journeyed to Europe and Africa. Fanon Che Wilkins has written that SNCC workers realized "as previous generations of black freedom activists had—that the problems that black folk faced in the United States extended far beyond the borders of Mississippi and Alabama."[5] They were able to interpret the leading world issues and crises of the day, such as the civil war in the Congo, the Berlin Wall, apartheid in South Africa, the Algerian revolution, and the Vietnam War through the lens of Cold War competition, and through recognizing how racism and imperialism functioned to maintain regimes of injustice.

showing Huey Newton sitting on a woven bamboo chair dressed in black pants and a leather jacket, his black beret at an angle on his head. The broad oval back of the chair that fans out behind him, the zebra skin rug at his feet, and the shields resting beside him all suggest Africa. In one hand Newton holds an African spear, and in the other a long rifle, overlaying an ancient regal style on his simple pose. The poster was made from a photograph that Eldridge took in the early Black Panther days, before Newton got arrested for a shooting that left one policeman dead and one wounded and landed in jail facing murder charges. Newton's case became the centerpiece of our dynamic "Free Huey" mobilization that catapulted the Black Panther movement across the country, and the popularity of that poster soared. The undulating horizontal bands of light and dark crossed by the rigid outline of the weapons that framed the portrait

of the intense young warrior gave a captivating energy to the poster, which took on a life of its own as it became a powerful symbol of our struggle.

Emory Douglas, after accompanying me from San Francisco to Algiers, had returned to California in order to prepare an exhibit of his art for the Pan-African Cultural Festival and come back as a member of the delegation. On the bare walls of our center he mounted the black-framed posters of martyred Black Panthers and boldly colored drawings of armed Afro Americans he brought back, graphically portraying our people's struggle. His drawings broke the language barrier and the Algerian onlookers reacted enthusiastically. On the tables inside we arranged stacks of our Black Panther newspaper, for which Emory designed the layout, along with other literature. Julia Wright Hervé, the daughter of the author Richard Wright, brought several

French-speaking Afro Americans from Paris with her to work at our center. I'd met her in Paris only days after leaving the U.S. in May, and she'd become an invaluable friend and supporter of our movement. In Algiers, she became an informal member of our delegation to the festival. The center opened on July 22, 1969, and despite the scorching heat, a crowd of African, Algerian, European, and American guests crammed inside and spilled out onto the sidewalk. In introducing the delegation to the audience, Julia Wright remarked that when Malcolm X came to Africa, he was only one man, but the Black Panthers had come to Africa as a fully developed organization representing the liberation struggle of Afro American people. The crowd gave an enthusiastic welcome to the Black Panther delegation, but during the comments and questions it was clear that Algerians were unfamiliar with our movement or the conditions we

> **" IN EVERY CITY I VISITED, I WAS STRUCK BY THE SIGHT OF BLACK POLICE OFFICERS, BLACK MEN BEHIND THE DESKS IN BANKS, BLACK PEOPLE NOT JUST ON BICYCLES BUT ALSO BEHIND THE WHEELS OF MERCEDES. BLACK PEOPLE IN CHARGE. BLACK PEOPLE DOING FOR _THEMSELVES_. "** —JOHN LEWIS

faced within the United States. That posed no barrier, however, to their understanding that American imperialism was a threat to their country and they warmly expressed solidarity with our opposition to it.

Eldridge and I, along with the entire Black Panther Party delegation, were housed in the elegant Hotel Aletti in the center of the city. The birth of our son Maceo on July 28, 1969, was announced in the daily newspaper _El Moudjahid_ and during the festival he became the center of lavish attention. Telegrams, letters, and flowers poured into the Afro-American Information Center and to our room at the Hotel Aletti. The telephone in our room rang constantly as family and friends called to share their joy at Maceo's birth. Well-wishers, supporters, and visitors to the festival drawn to the excitement surrounding Eldridge Cleaver and the Black Panthers flocked to our center. At the end of the

festival, our information center was closed, but visitors, acquaintances, people who wanted our participation in their projects, and friends from the U.S. continued to congregate in our hotel room. Our spacious bedroom with French doors opening onto a balcony overlooking the harbor seemed to shrink, while the incessant arrival of visitors and ringing of the telephone became nerve wracking. Julia came to my rescue again as I tried to recover from childbirth and take care of my infant son, gently steering the people insisting on meeting or interviewing Eldridge into a manageable pattern.

William Klein, a Paris-based American filmmaker whose documentary _Mohammed Ali: The Greatest_ gained him renown, was shooting the official film of the Pan-African Cultural Festival. Eldridge's friend and employer Robert Scheer, editor in chief of _Ramparts_ magazine, who had joined the cluster of visitors

drawn to Algiers during the festival, struck up a relationship with Klein. Scheer had persuaded Klein and the Algerian information ministry to collaborate with him on a documentary about Cleaver and the Black Panther struggle by the time I returned from the hospital with my new baby. While I spent my days inside the hotel caring for my infant son, a camera crew followed Eldridge and the Panthers around Algiers and filmed several days of Scheer interviewing Eldridge. Every surface became draped with cords, lights, and equipment when the film crew worked inside our hotel room. For publicity shots, a photographer had me and Eldridge pose on the balcony, standing in front of a huge blow up of his FBI wanted poster taped to the wall. One of the photographs, in which Eldridge is holding our son in his arms and I'm standing beside him, became the promotional poster for Klein's film

From left: Eldridge Cleaver, minister of information, David Hilliard, chief of staff, and Emory Douglas, minister of culture, attend a press conference with Palestinian delegates during the first Pan-African Cultural Festival, which took place in Algiers in July 1969. The Panthers opened an office there the following year. © Bruno Barbey/Magnum Photos.

———

Eldridge Cleaver: Black Panther. Klein later described his film as more abstract than documentary because of the need to censor information, since he didn't want anything he shot to be used by the FBI against Cleaver, who had sought refuge in Algiers because of criminal charges against him in the United States. Across the United States, the turbulent conflicts over the war in Vietnam or the racial violence at home hardly left any family untouched. Many people fled the United States, either young men who refused to fight in Vietnam or fugitives like Eldridge, determined not to be imprisoned for their participation in the black liberation movement. Klein's film brilliantly linked the guerrilla struggles for independence in Africa, the horrors of the Vietnam War, and the fight being waged within the United States by the Black Panther Party.

After returning to California, Scheer went about locating film footage about the Black Panthers for Klein's film, including local television coverage of a tense confrontation between Huey Newton and the San Francisco police right in front of the *Ramparts* office back in 1967. Particularly due to the commitment of a film collective known as Newsreel that had produced several short documentaries about the Black Panther Party in the San Francisco Bay Area, extensive material was available. Professional cameramen who belonged to Newsreel contributed talent and equipment after hours to produce these shorts, which captured the essential positions and activities of that moment in concise, memorable imagery. Their high-quality documentaries were made available to radical organizations and widely shown to win support and membership for the movement. In addition, European filmmakers had visited the

SNCC members were often received abroad with honors, and it encouraged them to see the civil rights struggle as embedded in the worldwide freedom movement. When Ahmed Sékou Touré, president of Guinea, decided to host a group of SNCC leaders who had been on the front lines of Freedom Summer in 1964, a group of eleven, including Julian Bond, John Lewis, Fannie Lou Hamer, Bob Moses, and James Forman boarded a plane for Conakry. Observing life in a black country was eye-opening for the group. John Lewis recalled, "With all the flying I'd done in the United States, this was the first time I'd ever seen black pilots. And that was just the beginning. In every city I visited, I was struck by the sight of black police officers, black men behind the desks in banks, black people not just on bicycles but also behind the wheels of Mercedes. Black people in charge. Black people doing for *themselves.*"[6]

In early 1966 SNCC took on U.S. foreign policy, arguing that it had "a right and a responsibility" to criticize it. It honed in on the interventions in Vietnam and the Dominican Republic and strongly rebutted the idea that civil rights groups should confine themselves to weighing in only on domestic affairs. The organization went further in wanting to extend foreign travel beyond the leadership circle to grassroots communities so that "people in the ghetto" could see a world beyond the parameters imposed on them by Jim Crow and "see the struggle in its entirety." In 1967 SNCC established an International Affairs Commission and used it to apply for nongovernmental organization status at the United Nations. The commission's

Bay Area to make documentaries about the Black Panthers, notably a young French woman named Agnes Varda, who arrived at the height of our mobilization around Newton's trial. Her film *Report on the Black Panthers* concluded with a shot of the shattered window of the Black Panther Party's national headquarters where Oakland police shot Huey Newton's poster in violent protest against the jury's failure to convict him of murder.

We loved Huey—he stood up to that racist terror every black community suffered, boldly and fearlessly, and lived to tell about it. Each of us drawn into the Black Panther Party, and the thousands we galvanized to support us, loved Huey. His trial and our mobilization to demand his release elevated him into a symbol of our movement. The details of his case weren't important; we just demanded he be set free. Our rallying cry became "Free Huey!" Although at the end of the trial he wasn't convicted of the capital offense of murder, he was not exonerated—and was convicted instead of manslaughter. We continued, both in court and in our mass rallies, to demand his freedom. On May 1, 1969, when a bail hearing was taking place in the federal court in San Francisco, we organized a huge demonstration in the plaza outside the building, which became the subject of a Newsreel documentary called *May Day.*

I designed the poster we used for that rally. In the center of a simple red star on a white field, I put a photograph of Huey, wearing his beret, his head slightly to the side, with a fierce expression on his face. The love we felt for Huey coursed through all our work, all our sacrifices, and the enthusiastic determination we showed in fighting to remove the crushing burden of racism from our people's lives. It bound those of us in our Black Panther Party so tightly we became like brothers and sisters, ready to lay down our lives for each other, ready to die for the struggle. We took seriously the injunction Stokely Carmichael gave when he spoke at the 1968 Huey Newton Birthday Rally, "We must have an undying love for our people!" What we meant was not that "turn the other cheek" kind of love, but a fervent commitment to defend and serve our communities, to liberate ourselves from the vicious bondage of the past. We fulfilled Che Guevara's observation that the true revolutionary is "guided by strong feelings of love." If a single jazz composition could epitomize the feelings of that moment in time, it would have to be the classic one we all admired and listened to over and over, John Coltrane's "A Love Supreme."

The Algerian authorities declined our request to open a Black Panther center, but after locating a place to live on the outskirts of Algiers, it became a base for the international operations—as well as a residence for our fluid commune of families and visitors—of the

LEFT: A crowd in the Afro-American Center views and buys posters by Black Panther Party minister of culture Emory Douglas. © Robert Wade. RIGHT: An Algerian woman at the International Branch of the Black Panther Party headquarters in Algiers, 1970. AP Photo.

Black Panther Party. By December, the North African sky turned grayer, the days grew cooler, and a damp chill blew into our windows from the Mediterranean Sea directly below. One afternoon, a long-distance call from the Black Panther headquarters brought grim news. In Chicago, Fred Hampton, the leader of our Illinois chapter, and Mark Clark, of our southern Illinois branch, had just been murdered in a police raid on the safe house where Hampton was sleeping around 4:00 a.m. on December 4. Eldridge stayed on the phone all day, talking with leaders of the Party around the country. His face was tense, his voice laced with anger. I felt numb, drained of life by the brutality of the killings and the terrible loss we sustained.

Before we could piece together the full story of the attack in Chicago, another deadly raid rocked our Party. The headquarters of the Los Angeles chapter was attacked in broad

daylight on December 8. A newly formed police unit called Special Weapons and Tactics (SWAT) mounted the assault, shooting for hours into the building on South Central Avenue. Geronimo, the defense minister who'd taken charge after the murder of Bunchy Carter that January, had made sure the offices were prepared, with sandbags, metal doors, and rooftop barricades. The Los Angeles police had shot into Geronimo's bedroom around dawn, but failed to hit him, and he was arrested before the daylight assault against our headquarters. All twelve or so Black Panthers inside were arrested after the shootout ended, but everyone called the Los Angeles raid a victory—because no one was killed!

We learned that these blatant attacks were triggering storms of protest. In Los Angeles, thousands of outraged black people flocked to the steps of the courthouse where the Panthers

were jailed; in Chicago, thousands of neighbors, supporters, and admirers of Fred Hampton filed through the apartment where the young leader was murdered in his sleep to mourn the destruction. This crisis accelerated the level of chaos within the Black Panther Party, but it pushed onlookers into becoming supporters, and supporters into taking action. The coordinated effort being waged by police and intelligence agencies to decimate the Panthers cast a brighter spotlight on us than ever before, and demands were rising around the country to stop the killing. *Life* magazine decided to run a story about the Black Panthers, and sent their star photojournalist Gordon Parks to Algiers to interview Eldridge.

Gordon Parks, a black man celebrated for his elegant photography, immediately seemed at ease visiting our apartment. He spoke to Eldridge as if they knew each other, unlike most journalists I'd

director, James Forman, formally addressed the General Assembly on November 17, 1967, on the subject of southern Africa. He described African Americans to the assembled delegates as an oppressed nation. Many liberals condemned SNCC for internationalizing the terms of the civil rights debate, but the failure of nonviolent direct action and "normal politics" to make effective changes reaffirmed the views of those who believed it imperative to seek foreign support.

Ever since the days of the Underground Railroad, Canada had figured in the black imaginary as both an antislavery ideal and a practical asylum. Even earlier, blacks who had fought with the British against the Americans in the Revolutionary War were evacuated to Canada along with other United Empire Loyalists once Britain conceded defeat. Their descendants, and Caribbean and African students and immigrants, formed the black communities of Canada. Following the independence of Jamaica, Barbados, and Trinidad and Tobago in the 1960s, Canada moved increasingly into the position of an economic hub for the Anglophone Caribbean. Like its neighbor to the south, the United States, it served as a target of migration, an axis of political influence, a source of investment capital in the island countries, and ultimately for Caribbean radicals, a neocolonial center.

The independence of the larger Caribbean states coincided with two other processes: the growth of civil rights insurgency in the United States and the independence of African

observed. The shock of the killings in Chicago had not worn off when he reached Algiers, and in conversation he seemed to share our grief, if not our revolutionary vision of transforming the United States. Eldridge was holding Maceo across his shoulder when Parks handed him a sheaf of newspaper clippings about the police attack against the Black Panthers in Chicago he'd brought with him. I was in the kitchen preparing dinner when Eldridge called me into the living room to take the baby. While he handed Maceo to me, I overheard him say, "It was cold-blooded murder, that's what it was," as Parks talked about the sympathy we were attracting as a result of Hampton's and Clark's deaths. "Sympathy won't stop bullets," Eldridge told him. At the dinner table, Parks told us he thought it was significant that Roy Wilkins, the NAACP leader, was forming a committee to investigate. None of us believed that would make any difference; we had already seen twenty-eight Panthers killed, and no police were ever held accountable for their deaths.

Parks came back to visit the next day and the day after, talking with Eldridge and taking photographs. He'd ask Eldridge, or me, to sit or stand in a certain place in the apartment. At one point during the session, he had Eldridge pose in a heavy, carved wooden chair, and then asked me to sit on the arm. Hanging on the wall above was the framed poster of Huey Newton I'd designed for the May Day rally that summer. Positioning his camera, Parks asked us to turn one way or another, rapidly clicking the whole time. When he was taking the picture (which we didn't see until months later when *Life* published his story), so much treachery was swirling around us I hardly gave any thought to what it might look like. But Parks brought an exquisite sense of composition and balance to his work, which made that photograph a particularly memorable one. He managed to capture the somber tone of our existence, the tense closeness of our marriage, and our devotion to the black liberation movement in one image. It was a portrait which merged the revolutionary with the traditional, captured that polarized, exhilarating, and deadly era we were living through in 1969, and imbued it with a timeless power.

former colonies. In the course of the 1960s citizens throughout Africa and the diaspora, especially the young, became increasingly disaffected with the leadership of their countries, the persistent economic inequality and underdevelopment in their nations, and the ongoing political power exerted by the former empires. They recognized that blacks in power did not necessarily equal black power.

In the United States, the 1966 advent of the Black Panther Party continued the internationalist focus associated with Malcolm X and SNCC. Established originally as a citizens' watchdog group in Oakland, California, by Huey Newton and Bobby Seale, the party broadened its focus beyond the issue of police brutality to embrace a substantial program of civil rights and social welfare reforms. Its awareness of struggles taking place outside

the African American community, its militancy and deliberately cultivated self-image, and its willingness to cooperate with other organizations put it in the international spotlight.

Two years after the party's founding the Black Panthers received an invitation from black Canadians in Halifax, Nova Scotia, to visit the city and describe their work. Nova Scotia, where fugitive slave soldiers from the American Revolution had settled, had not proven the sanctuary they had hoped for. Generations of poverty and discrimination plagued their progeny. Another invitation extended to the Panthers as well as to SNCC by students and faculty at Dalhousie University signaled the growing determination of Nova Scotians to compel change.

Black Power radicals in the United States visited other Canadian sites and there was

Israeli Black Panthers. The T-shirt reads "Black Panther" in Hebrew. © *Micha Bar-Am/ Magnum Photos.*

a flow back and forth across the border of militants exchanging ideas and strategies. This began to concern the Royal Canadian Mounted Police, who with the cooperation of the Federal Bureau of Investigation, began to monitor this communication. The 1967 insurrection in Detroit, just across from Windsor, Ontario, accelerated Canadian authorities' efforts to improve their intelligence and prevent Canada being drawn into the violent conflicts occurring in the United States. Growing discontent was also being expressed by Native Americans in the United States, First Nations aboriginal peoples in Canada, and Quebec separatists. Ensuring that these struggles remained separate was a clear imperative for the governments concerned.[7]

Cross-border Black Power in the United States and Canada reflected to some degree

The Afro-American Center opened by the Black Panther Party in Algiers during the Pan-African Cultural Festival. © Robert Wade.

SAMI SHALOM CHETRIT

My Black Panthers (in Israel)

I was almost eleven years old when the Israeli Black Panthers (inspired by the American movement) first took their social rage to the streets of Jerusalem in March 1971. We watched them on the evening news reports on our black-and-white TV, in our little public-housing apartment in Ashdod, at the time a working-class immigrant town. My father was inspired by those young men, mostly Moroccan immigrants, like us, for their courage, their determination, and their clear message: We want equality! Stop poverty!

It didn't take long for my father to organize the residents of our neighborhood into a demonstration for the improvement of our bad living conditions; we lived in a neighborhood that was rapidly becoming a slum. It happened all over Israel in communities like ours. People got the message and joined the wave of protest. Our demonstration was mainly about poor infrastructure, inadequate community services, and general neglect. I remember marching with hundreds of residents—men,

The realization that independence did not fulfill the hopes of the people contributed to the emergence of the Black Power movement in the Caribbean. The aftermath of a Black Power protest in Port of Spain, Trinidad, 1970. AP Photo.

———

women and children—to city hall, holding banners and yelling, "We want equality!" and more. We stopped in front of the city hall building and my father yelled demands into the megaphone in his hand, calling the mayor to come out and talk to the residents. Some people started throwing stones at the building. I heard glass break. My father begged people to stop any violent acts. I got scared. The police arrived and I ran away with my friends. Later that evening I was surprised to hear from my father that the mayor agreed to meet with a delegation of the residents to discuss improvements for our neighborhood infrastructure and services. It didn't make sense to me then as a child. Not too long after that my father joined the workers union and forgot about that demonstration. Then came the October (1973) War, which demolished the Panthers. It seems that we all forgot about them. I went to high school and developed interest in writing and soccer. Years went by.

Only many years after that experience, when I did my PhD research on the Black Panthers, did I learn that their aggressive demonstrations, sometimes violent and with many arrests, were very successful—they achieved big changes in the next government's budget, nicknamed the "Panthers' budget." All the allocations dealing with education, welfare, health, housing, and youth programs doubled, and some even tripled. That budget was issued only after a special committee for the investigation of poverty was formed to examine the issues brought up by the Panthers. The committee made recommendations to the government of Golda Meir to address, for the first time, the poor treatment of one million immigrants from the Middle East and North Africa.

Years after the movement became inactive I was fortunate to get to know its leaders.

unrest in Caribbean countries. In Trinidad members of the oilfield workers and sugar workers unions joined students in protesting the arrests in Canada of some Caribbean university students. The students were alleged to have trashed a mainframe computer at Sir George Williams University. While Canada was depicted as a neocolonial power, the direct target of the demonstrations was local: the government of Trinidadian prime minister Eric Williams. In spring 1970 the Black Power–inspired worker-student coalition nearly brought it down. As warships from Venezuela and the United States stood off Port of Spain, arson, bombings, and a wave of strikes reflected popular dissatisfaction with the status quo. The annual carnival became an occasion for protest, featuring posters of Malcolm X, Trinidad-born Stokely Carmichael (who had been barred from returning home), and Chinese Communist Party leader Mao Tse-tung.

Conflict occurred in other Caribbean countries whose leaders argued that Black Power made little sense in nations where blacks were already in charge. The same politicians nevertheless began to speak more aggressively about the roles played by foreign banks and corporations. Carmichael was finally allowed to visit the place of his birth. Guyana abandoned the periwigs traditionally used in British courts. In spite of the dread expressed by many Caribbean governments, Black Power in the region made moderate democratic demands for popular participation. Protesters criticized the commercial and political elites whose domination dated to colonial

I was inspired by their ongoing passion for action and by their modesty and to some extent naive attitude toward life: It was the end of the 1990s and they still believed in change. They still had faith in people and their ability to unite and mobilize. I simply fell in love.

During my graduate studies in Jerusalem, it became clear to me that I had a social duty to tell the story of the Black Panthers. I was an activist myself (among the founders of KEDMA, an alternative education movement, and HAKESHET, a social movement for change), and I regarded my research about the Mizrahi social struggle as yet another link in the struggle itself. I remember my frustration as I was working on my research (which came out in English as well: *Intra-Jewish Conflict in Israel: White Jews, Black Jews,* Routledge 2010) because I was having a hard time finding significant work about the Panthers. I couldn't stand the fact that Israeli historiography continued to push the Black Panthers' movement to the outermost margins of the Israeli historical narrative, largely labeling them as a negative episode that everyone would be better off forgetting. The challenge was to change the terminology itself: "struggle" instead of "riots," "oppressive relationships" and "racist policies" instead of "inferiority complex" and more. Decades after their initial emergence, only a handful of academic studies about the Israeli Black Panthers have been published and no documentary film has been made. I knew that I had to do something to bring their legacy back to life and reconnect their story and still-valid message with young activists and new movements for change.

The documentary film *The Black Panthers in Israel Speak,* which I produced and directed with my beloved friend, the late Eli Hamo (a young Panther himself during the 1970s), was in fact a by-product of my research on the Panthers. It started as interviews for my research but it soon became clear to us that it should be a film; a fifty-minute documentary had great potential to reach thousands of people in Israel and all over the world. It was almost a zero-budget production. It had no support of the main film foundations (except MAKOR foundation, which helped with postproduction) and most disappointingly, the film was rejected by all Israeli television stations—even to this day. We believed the film should become an educational tool for high schools, to be used as a trigger for classroom discussions about social and ethnic issues in Israel. Unfortunately I do not expect the educational system to deal officially with the Black Panthers movement or with the Mizrahi struggle in general, largely because I do not expect anything from such a system to begin with.

The larger question that

Israeli Black Panther demonstration in Jerusalem. Members of the Black Panthers were part of the Mizrahi community: Jews from North Africa and the Middle East who denounced and fought against the economic and cultural domination of the European Jews. © Micha Bar-Am/ Magnum Photos.

times. They wished to increase popular representation and disrupt neocolonial relationships that were rooted in the past. Black Power movements in North America contained intellectuals, both academic and organic, who were prepared to help envision societies that would be genuinely emancipatory. These included such figures as Trinidadian C.L.R. James, Malcolm X, and Guyanese Walter Rodney.[8]

Vigorous debates about the role of Marxism in the battle against racism and imperialism took place across the diaspora during the period. Major national liberation organizations in Angola, Mozambique, and Guinea-Bissau had defined themselves as socialist and revolutionary. Admirers of the Algerian revolution, the Panthers opened an information office in Algiers in 1970.

disturbed me in the 1990s was why Mizrahi researchers, writers, intellectuals, and organizations also chose to ignore the Black Panthers. After thirty years, many of these people were still afraid to identify with the Black Panthers' struggle, as if it were a private struggle carried out by a particular band of "not nice" youth (to use former Israeli prime minister Golda Meir's famous remark about them) from the Musrara neighborhood. Mizrahi politicians at the time loved to emphasize that "We are not Black Panthers," thus implying that in contrast to the Panthers, they were indeed "nice." All of that has changed. During the last decade and a half we have seen young Mizrahim directly identifying with the Black Panthers and even organizing in groups with names such as the "New Black Panthers" and the "Not Nice." We see more and more publications about the Panthers

and the struggle, we hear politicians using the language of the Panthers and even seeking their endorsement! I feel very privileged to have lived through this change, and even more so to have been a part of it.

Once again, from today's forty-five-year retrospective, and after engaging in thorough research of my own, I state without hesitation that the Black Panthers were the groundbreaking catalyst for the Mizrahi struggle in Israel. Israel before March 1971 was a different place than the Israel that followed. In the former, the economic and cultural oppression was accepted by Mizrahim with submissiveness, except for short rebellious outbursts that were repressed with an iron fist by the government and its Mizrahi collaborators, as in the case of the Wadi Salib uprising in 1959. The Panthers contributed to unmasking the economic and social relations in Israel, exposing a battlefield. Israel before the

appearance of the Black Panthers refused to admit its policy of inequality and denied its oppressive treatment of Mizrahim. Yet almost half a century later, Israel can no longer deny the economic and cultural oppression that today is becoming increasingly acute. The state is therefore in need of far more sophisticated mechanisms and means of manipulation than those of mere denial that it used in the past. Today, the increasing inequality is conspicuous in the undisguised war of the rich launched against any policy or self-organization of the Mizrahim aimed at addressing their sociopolitical woes. Of course, it is only a matter of time before the masses of oppressed workers fight back.

Alliances with Cuba, which was pursuing a foreign policy in Africa independent of the USSR, suggested to many that the future of these struggles did not have to be defined in the context of U.S.-Soviet rivalry. Some diaspora groups that modeled their own projects after African ones adopted the position that oppressed minorities in the metropolitan countries constituted an internal colony. As such, they might pursue aims that were political and/or culturally nationalist, as did, for a time, Amiri Baraka's (LeRoi Jones) Newark-based Kawaida enterprise. The issue of race, however, problematized Marxism both in Africa and abroad. Conventional Marxist-Leninism had not theorized it, and the failure to achieve clarity about what it was and meant for freedom movements ultimately lessened its impact while driving divisions within Black Power movements.

The interplay, both ideological and chronological, between Black Power insurgency in the United States, Canada, and the Caribbean indicates that studying it holistically as a North American phenomenon might be fruitful. As we examine Black Power from an even broader geographic perspective, national borders dissolve and allow us to see commonalities as well as differences.

———

The Black Power movement in Great Britain was galvanized by events in the United States. Its members were young Caribbean immigrants or children of immigrants. Stokely Carmichael gave a speech in London in 1967 that contributed to the launch of the movement. Black Panther demonstration in London, 1971. © Neil Kenlock.

Black Power became global, part of narratives of commerce, migration, imperialism, and cultural exchange.

Black Power symbolism, practices, and discourses were also mobilized outside of the North American continent. In Israel, an organization calling itself the Black Panther Party was composed of so-called Oriental Jews, those who had come to Israel from North Africa or other Middle Eastern countries rather than from Europe or the United States. There was no link between the Black Panther Party of Israel and the American one. Israeli Panthers had no revolutionary aspirations. They instead mounted protests against the discrimination they faced in Israel as representatives of groups widely perceived by European-descended Jews (Ashkenazim) as backward. The sons and daughters of more recent immigrants, many grew up in slum areas where drug use, crime, and educational failures were not uncommon. Israeli Panthers lashed out against menial employment, police brutality, and social marginalization. Racialization of these often swarthy North African and Middle Eastern Jews rankled their sensibilities. In these respects, they shared issues with American Panthers, but they made it clear that they were not internationalists. They were instead avid supporters of Israel's policies toward Arabs and the Arab states.[9]

Israeli Panthers considered bringing their issues to the attention of American Jews, seeking to divert some of the resources that that group offered primarily to Ashkenazim. One supporter of a proposed U.S. tour promised to provide aid if the Israeli Panthers would agree not to contact their American namesakes. The trip was eventually canceled but the Israeli Panthers had made their point. They positioned themselves as critics of alienation and discrimination based on ethnic heritage while reaffirming their patriotic identification with Israel. The Israeli Panthers had borrowed the imagery and trope of militancy of the U.S. Black Panthers to pursue a very different agenda. Their African American forbears had provided them with a highly adaptable repertoire with which they forced themselves into the consciousness of their nation.

That the Black Power imaginary could take on different meanings was manifested in India. Over the centuries, the elaboration of caste in Indian society led to refined distinctions among occupational and social groups and to the identification of those perceived as not being wholly legitimate members of society at all. These included the Dalits, excluded altogether from the caste system, confined to the most demeaning labor, subject to poverty and gross social discrimination, and deprived of

LEFT: Anti-imperialism march on African Liberation Day, Washington, DC, May 1974. © Risasi Zachariah Dais. MIDDLE: Children of the Black Power movement in Brixton, South London, 1971. © Neil Kenlock. RIGHT: Queen Mother Moore (left) and Amina Baraka (right) at a women's workshop during the 1974 conference of the African Liberation Support Committee, founded at a Black Power conference in Detroit in 1972. The ALSC conference gathered participants from twenty-seven states and six countries. © Risasi Zachariah Dais.

the benefits of community participation. Hinduism associated the Dalits with sin committed in past lives, and with bodily and spiritual pollution. Danger was embodied in the very person of the pariah.

Imperialist ideologies made it possible to see caste as it operated in India and other societies through the lens of race. The story of the Aryan conquest of India and the construction of a stratified society harmonized with the color-coded domination that Western empire builders carried with them to Africa and Asia. Slavery, and then colonialism, added additional layers of hierarchical authority to the social matrices experienced by peoples who fell under the control of the great powers. Scholars have documented the ways that racialist thought abetted the naturalization of white supremacy in the Western world and helped justify its conquests elsewhere. They have also studied the particular relationships between African Americans and Indians where the nexus was struggle against colonialism and racism. Much has been written about the influence of Gandhian nonviolent direct action on the civil rights movement.

Even earlier, World War I helped unleash the energies of Indian reformers who began opposing caste and challenging its claims to antiquity. One of these, Bhimrao Ramji Ambedkar, was a Dalit who with elite

sponsorship arrived at New York's Columbia University in 1913 to study with the philosopher John Dewey and the economist Edwin R.A. Seligman. Ambedkar was an admirer of Booker T. Washington's prescriptions for elevating oppressed peoples. Political experiences had made him skeptical of Indian nationalists' motives regarding Dalits, and he avoided participation in pro-independence groups while in America, not wishing to be distracted from his objective of acquiring the credentials that would propel him to leadership at home.

As a Columbia student attending classes within walking distance of the growing Harlem ghetto, Ambedkar understood the dynamics of race and color in the United States and carefully distinguished caste from these. "European students of caste have unduly emphasized the role of colour in the caste system," he noted. "Themselves impregnated by colour prejudices, they very readily imagined it to be the chief factor in the caste problem. But nothing can be further from the truth."[10] Caste and race shared some characteristics but they were not identical.

When Ambedkar returned home, he wrote that the causes of India's subjection to Britain lay in its premodern vulnerabilities. Caste retarded social and economic development. Dalits would never achieve power under colonialism nor

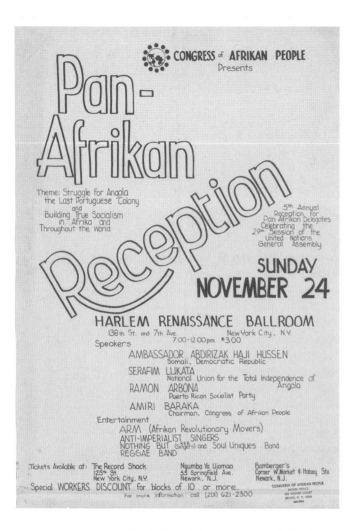

Flyer for a 1974 Pan-African reception organized by the Congress of African People in honor of the armed struggle in Angola against Portuguese colonialism. Angola, Mozambique, and Guinea-Bissau gained their independence from Portugal in 1975. Art and Artifact Division, Schomburg Center for Research in Black Culture, The New York Public Library.

would a simple transition to independence necessarily improve their lives. Sovereignty for India would only affirm upper caste domination. Pariah groups therefore would have to support national independence while struggling within its framework for human rights.

India became independent in 1947 and in January 1950 adopted a constitution designed to give relief to outcasts, the so-called "scheduled classes." The document, drafted in large part by Ambedkar, was challenged almost immediately. The Indian high court ruled that a professional school's special admissions process violated constitutional clauses granting equality to all citizens and protecting them from discrimination. India thus had its equivalent to the *Bakke* case twenty-seven years before litigants brought suit against minority preference policies in the United States. Unlike America, however, the parliament responded to the high court's finding not by limiting the scope of minority set-asides, but by amending the constitution to broaden the government's capacity to create them.

In spite of these efforts, the Indian government made insufficient headway against caste discrimination in the first decades of its independence. As a result, Dalit assertiveness developed, spearheaded by the postindependence second generation that had benefited from education but remained stymied by discrimination. In 1972 the Dalit Panthers of India (DPI) emerged as a militant response to the continuing status quo. The DPI consciously modeled itself on the American example. At first the organization adopted Ambedkar's disaffiliation with mainstream Indian politics, which had been inadequate to resolve Dalits' pressing problems, especially in rural areas. Later splinter factions moved toward a Marxist approach, seeking to include other low-status groups in a broad class analysis of caste.[11]

The global reach of Black Power politics extended to Australia in the late 1960s. The native peoples of Australia were in the unhappy position of being simultaneously an aboriginal community deprived of land rights and a racial minority deprived of civil rights. Developments in other countries, such as the freedom movement in the United States and decolonization in Africa had led to a growing awareness on the part of the Australian government that many of its policies, including the ban on immigrants of color, were out of step with the direction of world history. This realization did not result in immediate changes. Aborigines continued to struggle with encroachments on traditional lands by mining companies with the blessings of the government.

Growing demands for self-determination for native communities coincided with Black Power initiatives in other countries and with the United Nations' International Year for Action to Combat Racism and Racial Prejudice in 1971. Black Australian spokespersons traveled abroad between 1970 and 1972 and publicized aboriginal issues as they held meetings with both Black Power activists and indigenous leaders in the Americas. A small Black Panther chapter was founded in Brisbane. Actions by Black Power militants in Australia contributed to the election in 1972 of a Labor Party government that pledged to ensure land rights and self-determination for aboriginal communities.

Black Power took a variant form in Australia's neighbor, New Zealand. There, Polynesian immigrants from other Pacific islands and the native Maori people formed the core of insurgency. Added to the issues of control of native lands and racial equality were questions surrounding the rights and identities of newcomers. Like other practitioners of Black Power politics, New Zealanders derived lessons from the writings of Malcolm X and Huey Newton and attempted to apply these to their own circumstances.[12]

Black Power was an international movement that, in voicing common elements within the experiences of African and Africa-descended diaspora peoples, provided a framework that helped define their grievances and goals. Additionally, it supplied a vocabulary to others who, though spatially and culturally removed from the conditions of African diaspora life, and engaged in struggles with different objectives, found meaning in the interpretations conceived through Black Power's set of values and practices. Proponents in Asia, the Middle East, and Oceania borrowed from the movement's rich cultural and political inventory to shape their own agendas in response to local conditions. Black Power's legacy is the ongoing history of the worldwide determination to contest all forms of domination and injustice.

"GROWING DEMANDS FOR SELF-DETERMINATION FOR NATIVE COMMUNITIES COINCIDED WITH BLACK POWER INITIATIVES IN OTHER COUNTRIES AND WITH THE UNITED NATIONS' INTERNATIONAL YEAR FOR ACTION TO COMBAT RACISM AND RACIAL PREJUDICE IN 1971."

Young girl with Afro and African-inspired tunic, carrying a black doll and a book of "black autographs." Oakland, 1968. Bob Fitch Photography Archive, © Stanford University Libraries, Department of Special Collections.

CHAPTER 7

Black Power: The Looks

Jeffrey O.G. Ogbar

Fashion was the most immediate and obvious marker of Black Power's influence. Many younger African Americans, regardless of the degree to which they were politically active, donned Afros, African-inspired clothes, or sartorial inflections of militancy, often associated with organized black nationalist or revolutionary organizations. Fashion was a clear declaration of what some called the "new black mood," which swept Black America. The fundamental thrust of Black Power was black self-determination, and a very clear affirmation of black people's humanity. To that end, racial pride was inextricably tied to the cosmetics of blackness.

Nothing, of course, comes out of a vacuum. The rise of these new fashions was a consequence of many factors, including the steady growth of black nationalism in the years leading up to 1966. Typically, black nationalists celebrated the beauty of black people and addressed the psychological trauma of being black in a racist society that essentially viewed the concept of black beauty as oxymoronic. While civil rights activists discussed the deleterious effects of white supremacy, there was very little, if any, conversation about celebrating black beauty or African history.

Since the nineteenth century, black nationalists had conspicuously celebrated African physical features as beautiful and stressed the importance of reclaiming African history, and, in some cases, African attire. By the early 1960s, no advocate for black nationalism was as well known as Malcolm X, the national spokesman for the Nation of Islam, the largest black nationalist organization in the United States. Black self-love and the politics of black beauty were consistent themes in Malcolm's speeches.

COSMETICS

Black nationalist organizations such as the Nation of Islam had long derided cosmetics designed to whiten the skin or straighten the hair. The Nation's spokesman, Malcolm X, frequently addressed the difficulty many black people had with reconciling racial pride and living in an antiblack society. In 1963, he asked an audience, "Who taught you to hate the color of your skin? Who taught you to hate the texture of your hair? Who taught you to hate the shape of your nose and the shape of your lips? Who taught you to hate yourself from the top of your head to the soles of your feet? Who taught you to hate your own kind?" And beyond a categorical chastening of black people for their love

> **"YEARS BEFORE THE BLACK POWER MOVEMENT ... SMALL NUMBERS OF VISIBLE BLACK WOMEN WHO WERE PROFESSIONAL DANCERS, AND SOME SINGERS SUCH AS ABBEY LINCOLN, STARTED TO WEAR NATURAL, UNSTRAIGHTENED HAIR. THIS CHOICE WAS A CLEAR DEPARTURE FROM THE CULTURAL STANDARDS OF THE WIDER BLACK COMMUNITY AND CAUSED A SENSE OF ALARM FOR SOME."**

affair with white standards of beauty, the minister also conspicuously ridiculed the concept of white beauty itself.

Reflecting the Nation of Islam's general message regarding whiteness, Malcolm spoke humorously to captivated black audiences about how "ignorant Negroes" had been so in love with white people that they endured painful cosmetic rituals to approximate their oppressors' "animal-like" appearance. Negroes rubbed toxic ointments onto their skin to whiten it. They wanted the complexion of the "pig-colored" white man. They wanted to have a nose like the long "snout" of the white man. Negroes even wanted the "dog-like" hair of the white man. Malcolm personalized his message by discussing his own love affair with white standards of beauty. When he got his first process, he recalled that it was "my first really big step toward self-degradation: when I endured all of that pain, literally burning my flesh to have it look like a white man's hair. I had joined that multitude of Negro men and women in America who are brainwashed into believing that the black people are 'inferior'—and white people 'superior'—that they will even violate and mutilate their God-created bodies to try to look 'pretty' by white standards."

Malcolm touched a nerve with these speeches. For generations black people had been told they were incapable, insufficient, unattractive, unworthy, and unfit. Through a host of media and cultural artifacts, they were told that they were ugly. Vicious stereotypes depicted black men and women as grotesque figures in movies, cartoons, advertisements for household products, tourist postcards, and popular sayings. One such saying even circulated in the black community:

> *If you're white, you're alright*
> *If you're yellow, you're mellow*
> *If you're brown, stick around*
> *If you're black, get back!*

Kinky hair and dark skin were widely stigmatized, even among black people. In fact, dark skin was generally held in such low regard that calling someone "black" was tantamount to a pejorative. When making reference to skin color, people would use words considered more innocuous: "sepia," "tan," "café au lait," and even "brown" as alternative markers of blackness. Kinky hair was derisively called "nappy" and unmanageable, while curly or wavy texture was known as "good hair." To address this widely accepted sense of beauty (or lack thereof), entire cosmetic industries

Grandassa Models (from Grandassaland, the name Carlos A. Cooks gave to the landmass once formed by Africa and Asia) were founded in 1962. They came out of the Miss Natural Standard of Beauty Contest held yearly during Garvey Day by Cooks and the African Nationalist Pioneer Movement. Natural beauty, jazz, African liberation, and politics were important features of Grandassa Models. New York. 1968. © Kwame Brathwaite.

emerged to cater to African Americans' desires to change their appearance.

African Americans also lightened their skin with a range of chemicals and ointments. In fact, skin whitening was so ubiquitous that advertisements for such products were an important part of revenue in the black press. The Baltimore *Afro-American* newspaper, for example, generated a fifth of its advertisement profits from these ads. From the pages of the *Chicago Defender, Pittsburgh Courier,* or the *Los Angeles Sentinel,* to magazines like *Ebony* and *Sepia,* skin-whitening advertisements were common. In fact, only black nationalist newspapers like the *Negro World,* the *Black Man,* or *Muhammad Speaks,* didn't carry them. By the late 1960s, however, a conspicuous shift occurred in the black press.

Years before the Black Power movement,

however, among non-nationalists in the early 1960s, small numbers of visible black women who were professional dancers, and some singers such as Abbey Lincoln, started to wear natural, unstraightened hair. This choice was a clear departure from the cultural standards of the wider black community and caused a sense of alarm for some. For many, the look was bizarre. Yet for others, it was an aesthetic connection with women in African countries who were increasingly visible as independence movements gained more attention in the U.S.—natural hair simultaneously affirmed racial pride and political consciousness.

In 1966, Stokely Carmichael insisted that black people "have to stop being ashamed of being black. A broad nose, a thick lip, and nappy hair is us and we are going to call that beautiful whether they like it or not. We are not

going to fry our hair anymore." As the movement matured, the natural hairstyle grew into a larger round-shaped style that became known as an Afro. This was an obvious connection with Africa, though the style was essentially an African American creation. In many respects, the Afro was an even bolder statement of black pride, a metaphorical exclamation point, affirming the beauty of black people and their hair. The new generation of poets, musicians, and visual artists in the Black Arts Movement addressed this new celebration of black natural beauty in creative ways. In a 1969 poem, "Natural Black Beauty," Joe Goncalves explained black beauty: "Our lips complement our noses, our noses 'go with' our eyes, and they all bless our skin, which is black. If your face does not complement itself, you are in a degree of trouble. . . . The real geometry of our faces, the natural geometry in terms of art is found, among other places, in African sculpture. Our natural architecture, our natural rhythm."

Hair, much like skin color, had been part of a long, often painful, cultural and social milieu around beauty, femininity, and black women. For many black women, the transition to natural hair was a much more difficult and substantive act than for men, who were generally not pressured to make cosmetic adjustments to "correct nature's mistakes." Embracing natural hair was tied to notions of self-worth, racial pride, and simultaneously one's place in a given social space. Historian Robin D.G. Kelley explains that the Afro was not only "a valorization of blackness . . . but a direct rejection of a female beauty that many black men themselves had upheld."

In 1969 *Ebony,* which had been the major lifestyle periodical for African Americans, published a special issue on the "Black Revolution," which included an essay by Black Arts poet Larry Neal. The poet discussed the power of black beauty as more than aesthetics, but an essential complement to the wider political struggle for the liberation of black people. "For a Sister to wear her hair natural asserts the

Embracing natural hair was tied to notions of self-worth and racial pride. The Committee for Racial Pride of the Grandassa Models pickets Wigs Parisian, a Harlem store, in 1963. © Klytus Smith. Photographs and Prints Division, Schomburg Center for Research in Black Culture, The New York Public Library.

sacred and essentially holy nature of her body. The natural, in its most positive sense, symbolizes the Sister's willingness to determine her own destiny. It is an act of love for herself and her people. The natural helps to psychologically liberate the Sister. It prepares her for the message of a Rap Brown, a Robert Williams, a Huey Newton, a Maulana Karenga."

In Neal's poem, the shift toward the natural as a hairstyle was simultaneously an affirmation of black women and their beauty. In fact, much of the emphasis on black beauty was a celebration of black women as beautiful in a society where they were held against white standards of beauty. But as scholar Margo Natalie Crawford notes, this "poem fully unveils the male gaze that often shaped Black Arts Movement formulations of 'natural black beauty' and the Black Arts Movement equation of 'natural' beauty and dark-skinned blackness." Crawford continues, "unfortunately, Neal does not imagine that the 'Sister with the Natural' might be more drawn to

Audrey Lorde's poem 'Naturally' (1970)." And in addition to male gaze, the poem, like much of the work that celebrated the shift to the natural hairstyle, overlooked how much the shift also affected black men.

For decades many black men, particularly working-class and poor urban men, chemically straightened their hair with conks or perms, much in the way that women did. Although it was significantly more common among poor and working-class black men, black musicians in rock and roll and R & B also donned conks: Chuck Berry, Little Richard, Fats Domino, Ike Turner, Smokey Robinson, James Brown, the Isley Brothers, Nat King Cole, Wilson Pickett, the Temptations, and others. While middle-class

TOP LEFT: The valorization of blackness and black aesthetics reflected a "new black mood." Blackstone Nation graffiti, Chicago. © Darryl Cowherd. TOP RIGHT: Kathleen Cleaver (left) and fellow Black Panthers sporting Afros. Oakland. 1968 © Stephen Shames. BOTTOM LEFT: The urban black militants' attire consisted of dark sunglasses, black leather jackets, and Afros. The Panthers, among others, thought that African connections through clothes, for example, did not reflect the revolutionary consciousness of urban blacks. Panthers in Defermery Park, Oakland. 1968 © Stephen Shames. BOTTOM RIGHT: Stokely Carmichael, at a Panther rally, wears the Panther black leather jacket, but true to his Pan-Africanist vision, he also wears a dashiki. Like him, and in contrast to Panthers elsewhere, members of the New York chapter of the Party often wore African-inspired clothes. Oakland, 1968. Bob Fitch Photography Archive, © Stanford University Libraries, Department of Special Collections.

———

black men did not straighten their hair, they generally wore their hair cropped very close to the head by the 1950s and 1960s. Men like Dr. Martin Luther King Jr., for example, had hairstyles identical to their fathers.

One of the earliest and most visible shifts toward a natural hairstyle among black popular singers came from Sam Cooke, often called the father of soul music. Cooke departed from the conks typical of black male singers. Moreover, his natural hair grew longer between 1960 and 1964, almost in anticipation of the Afro styles that would emerge a few years later. Beyond his hairstyle, Cooke was also connected to the black freedom movement, producing the iconic song, "A Change Is Gonna Come" in 1964, as well as being friends with Malcolm X and Cassius Clay. By the late 1960s, younger black males across different class backgrounds embraced the Afro. Bastions of black elite society, like King's alma

mater Morehouse College, featured students with Afros, and homecoming courts featuring Spelman students from some of the most prominent black families with Afros. By the end of the decade, it was clear that a generation of African Americans had embraced a radically new aesthetic.

When he became the world's heavyweight champion in February 1964, Clay celebrated with Cooke in the ring and soon after declared his membership in the Nation of Islam and his new name, Muhammad Ali. Known to the world as a bold, defiant black-nationalist figure, Ali did something that no black male popular figure had done heretofore: he simultaneously offered a bold resistance to white supremacy while celebrating his own black beauty. By the close of the decade, black male singers embraced the Afro writ large. Groups like the Four Tops, the Temptations, the Isley Brothers, as well as new groups such as the

TOP LEFT: Republic of New Afrika's Chokwe Lumumba and his wife, Anasa, in African-inspired clothes. 1974. Detroit News Collection/Walter P. Reuther, Archives of Labor and Urban Affairs, Wayne State University. TOP RIGHT: Young Black Panthers. Oakland. 1968 Bob Fitch Photography Archive, © Stanford University Libraries, Department of Special Collections. BOTTOM: Panthers in urban militant uniform. Oakland, 1968. © Stephen Shames.

Jackson Five, the Chi-Lites, and Sly and the Family Stone adorned their heads with crowns of bold blackness. In some respects, the Afro was not just a declaration of black pride, it was simply cool. By the late 1960s, black female singers similarly adopted natural hairstyles. From Nina Simone and Aretha Franklin to Diana Ross and the Supremes, natural hair conveyed beauty in a way not previously witnessed in the United States.

These new styles were so pervasive that they permeated non–African American social and cultural spaces as well. In New York City, Puerto Ricans—who had lived alongside African Americans for decades—began sporting Afros. The rise of Black Power had helped foment a cultural and political shift among Puerto Rican activists and the wider community.

In 1967 a predominantly Puerto Rican Chicago street gang, the Young Lords Organization, led by Jose (Cha Cha) Jimenez, entered into a formal alliance with the local Black Panther Party, declaring itself a revolutionary nationalist organization dedicated to the liberation of Puerto Ricans on the mainland and the island. In its footsteps, the Young Lords Party was launched in New York City in 1969. Young Lords chapters opened in Bridgeport, Connecticut, Philadelphia, and Newark.

Much like other militant groups of their era, the Young Lords understood that the power of oppression had a cultural component. Liberation movements, therefore, needed a cultural component that subverted the intentions of the oppressor. To that end, the Afro was a proud inversion of the long tradition to straighten hair and avoid any appearance of having *pelo malo,* or "bad hair." Major leaders of the Lords, such as Felipe Luciano and Pablo "Yoruba" Guzman, sported Afros that conspicuously brought attention to their African ancestry in ways that were a salient rejection of copious efforts to minimize its visibility. Some Lords even remarked about how shocked family members were to see them grow Afros when they had worked so hard to straighten their hair.

But the cultural shifts among Puerto Rican or African American young people were not limited to cosmetics, of course. Fashions in attire were ubiquitous and took many creative forms. There arose urban militant chic as well as African-inspired cultural nationalist styles that pervaded the sartorial landscape.

FASHION

Fashion was inextricably tied to the impulse of Black Power. Still, there was no agreement, even among Black Power advocates, on whether certain sartorial expressions were even beneficial to black people. Cultural nationalists, for example, understood culture in general, and fashion in particular, as a very important statement of self-determination, dignity, and racial pride. The *buba,* or dashiki, emerged in great popularity, even among people who were not often organized nationalists or activists. The homecoming courts of many historically black colleges and universities often donned African-inspired clothing. The Fashion Fair Company, a subsidiary of Johnson Publishing, featured models with African-print styles. It was not uncommon to see dancers on the popular Soul Train television show with dashikis. Maulana Karenga, the co-founder and leader of the Us Organization, a black-nationalist group based in Los Angeles, noted that clothing, like names, holidays, and other rituals, was an essential ingredient to the liberation of black people where culture was central. Liberation would remain elusive, "unless [black people are] imbued with cultural values."

While fashion, for many, was a clear measure of one's political orientation, it was also a dynamic metric. Even the civil rights movement had grappled with the politics of fashion. In the early 1960s, activists often dressed in "respectable" attire at demonstrations, wearing suits, ties, and dresses. By the mid-1960s, the most militant of the leading civil rights organizations, the Student Nonviolent Coordinating Committee (SNCC), began wearing overalls as a way to identify with the local people with whom they worked in the rural South. By 1966, however, even SNCC leadership dressed as had urban black militants: dark sunglasses, jean or black leather jackets, and Afros.

Masai Hewitt, minister of education for the Black Panther Party, clearly embraced significant elements of cultural nationalism, in his name change to Masai and his wearing dashikis. It is clear that the Panthers as well as a range of Black Power organizations large and small, such as the African Nationalist Pioneer Movement in New York, the

The Black Panther Party was critical of cultural nationalism and its African-inspired clothes, but this Panther mixed the leather jacket and beret with an "African" necklace. Oakland, 1968. Bob Fitch Photography Archive, © Stanford University Libraries, Department of Special Collections.

> **" BY THE WANING YEARS OF THE BLACK POWER MOVEMENT, AFRICAN AMERICANS HAD BEEN INDELIBLY AFFECTED BY THE FUNDAMENTAL GOAL OF SELF-LOVE, RACIAL PRIDE, AND COMMUNITY AFFIRMATION. "**

African Descendants Nationalist Independent Party (AD NIP) in Portland and Seattle, the Us Organization, and the Congress of African People (CAP), understood the politics of fashion. The Black Panther Party, however, was openly critical of fashion as a marker of political consciousness, or even a tool of political resistance. In fact, the Party argued that cultural nationalism itself was politically impotent in confronting the daunting forces of oppression. Linda Harrison, a member of the BPP and journalist for the *Black Panther* newspaper, argued that. "Those who believe in the 'I'm Black and I'm Proud' theory believe that there is a dignity inherent in wearing naturals; that a buba makes a slave a man; and that a common language—Swahili—makes all of us brothers." Instead, Harrison insisted, the oppressive system "condones and even worships this new pride which it uses to sell every product under the sun. It worships and condones anything that is harmless and presents no challenge to the existing order."

In a similar vein, Fred Hampton, deputy chairman of the Illinois chapter of the Black Panther Party, urged a crowd to "check the people [who] are wearing dashikis and bubas and think that that's going to free them. Check all of these people, find out where they are located . . . write them a letter and ask them in the last year how many times has their office been attacked. And then write the Black Panther Party,

anywhere in the United States of America . . . and ask them [the same question.]. That's when you figure out what the pigs don't like." Despite these criticisms, the Panthers intuitively understood the power of culture and its intersection with fashion and politics. Their choice of an urban militant style demonstrated this clearly, even if the BPP also understood that their politics could not be reduced to their uniform.

The Panthers adopted the black beret in 1966. It was part of an ensemble that included styles that had already organically become popular among urban black militants across the country: black leather jacket, sunglasses, and black slacks. Under the beret, of course, was a proud coif of natural hair. David Sanchez, founder of the largely Chicano Brown Berets, found inspiration in the ideology as well as the sartorial style of the Black Panthers. Sanchez declared that the brown color of his group's beret represented the "dignity and pride in the color of my skin and my race." The Young Lords Party similarly donned berets as part of its official uniform.

During the Summer Olympic Games of 1968, three African Americans swept the 400-meter race and, in solidarity with the global struggle for black liberation, donned black berets. Lee Evans, one of the three winners, explained that their choice of beret was not random, but tied to the most visible of the black militant groups in the U.S. "Black berets then were worn by the Black Panthers.

TOP: The Congress of African People, a cultural nationalist group, believed in armed self-defense and a politics beyond the dashiki. Women at the 1972 Congress of African People summit in San Diego. Photographs and Prints Division, Schomburg Center for Research in Black Culture, The New York Public Library. BOTTOM LEFT: During the 1968 Olympics Lee Evans (gold), Larry James (silver), and Ronald Freeman (bronze) won the 400-meter race and, in solidarity with the struggle for black liberation, donned black berets. Evans later explained, "Black berets then were worn by the Black Panthers. I wanted to show black pride." AP Photo/ stf. BOTTOM RIGHT: Republic of New Afrika co-founder Imari Abubakari Obadele (Richard Henry) and a member of the RNA in military-style uniform. In a nod to Africa, the military jacket's epaulettes imitate leopard skin. 1969. Detroit News Collection/Walter P. Reuther, Archives of Labor and Urban Affairs, Wayne State University.

I wanted to show black pride." Even unorganized street youth wore the beret and other elements of the Panther uniform. One Panther noted that "although this imitation made us feel rather proud, one had difficulty discerning Oakland youth from Panthers."

The beret had become a major icon of militancy and political consciousness, as well as simple chic fashion. Radicals in Latino, white, Native, and Asian American communities similarly donned berets. And despite their vitriolic condemnation of cultural nationalism, the Black Panther Party fundamentally understood the utility of culture as an affirming force for the people. Whether expressed by groups like AD NIP, Us, CAP, or even the Republic of New Africa, the urban militant styles of the black leather jacket, dark sunglasses, Afro, and beret were clear markers of a subversive sartorial expression. It was part of the core thrust of Black Power.

By the waning years of the Black Power movement, African Americans had been indelibly affected by the fundamental goal of self-love, racial pride, and community affirmation. "Black" was no longer a fighting word. The black press was no longer full of advertisements encouraging readers to get their skin as white as possible. Natural hair on black people was not viewed as bizarre. Universal pride in blackness (however it could be quantified) remained elusive, but no moment had pushed black people closer to it than this era. It was one of the many ways that Black Power substantively shaped the cultural landscape of the United States.

BIBLIOGRAPHY

Banks, Ingrid. *Hair Matters: Beauty, Power and Black Women's Consciousness* (New York: New York University Press, 2000).

Baraka, Amiri, and Larry Neal, eds. *Black Fire: An Anthology of Afro-American Writing* (Baltimore, MD: Black Classic Press, 2007).

Bracey Jr., John H., Sonia Sanchez, and James Smethurst. *SOS Calling All Black People: A Black Arts Movement Reader* (Amherst: University of Massachusetts Press, 2014).

Clark, Cheryl. *"After Mecca": Women Poets and the Black Arts Movement* (New Brunswick, NJ: Rutgers University Press, 2004).

Collins, Lisa Gail, and Margo Natalie Crawford. *New Thoughts on the Black Arts Movement* (New Brunswick, NJ: Rutgers University Press, 2006).

Joseph, Peniel E. *Waiting 'Til the Midnight Hour: A Narrative History of Black Power in America* (New York: Holt, 2007).

Ogbar, Jeffrey O.G. *Black Power: Radical Politics and African American Identity* (Baltimore, MD: Johns Hopkins University Press, 2005).

Ongiri, Amy Abugo. *Spectacular Blackness: The Cultural Politics of the Black Power Movement and the Search for a Black Aesthetic* (Charlottesville: University of Virginia Press, 2009).

Smethurst, James Edward. *The Black Arts Movement: Literary Nationalism in the 1960s and 1970* (Chapel Hill: University of North Carolina Press, 2005).

Widener, Daniel. *Black Arts West: Culture and Struggle in Postwar Los Angeles* (Durham, NC: Duke University Press, 2010).

CONTRIBUTOR BIOGRAPHIES

Muhammad Ahmad co-founded the Afrikan People's Party in the 1970s and the Revolutionary Action Movement in the 1960s. He has worked with the National Association for the Advancement of Colored People (NAACP), the Congress of Racial Equality (CORE), the Student Nonviolent Coordinating Committee (SNCC), and the Black Panther Party.

Dan Berger is the author of *Captive Nation: Black Prison Organizing in the Civil Rights Era; The Struggle Within: Prisons, Political Prisoners, and Mass Movements in the United States;* and *Outlaws of America: The Weather Underground and the Politics of Solidarity.* He is the editor of *The Hidden 1970s: Histories of Radicalism* and *Letters from Young Activists: Today's Rebels Speak Out.* Berger teaches comparative ethnic studies at the University of Washington, Bothell.

Sami Shalom Chetrit is a poet, writer, filmmaker, and activist. He studied at the Hebrew University of Jerusalem and Columbia University and teaches at Queens College. He was among the founders and leaders of KEDMA, the association for equal education in Israel, and Hakeshet, a Mizrahi social movement. He is the author of numerous articles and books on ethnic relations, culture, society, education, and the Israeli-Palestinian conflict.

Kathleen Neal Cleaver joined the Student Nonviolent Coordinating Committee in 1967, and has continued to engage in human rights work to free wrongfully imprisoned activists and to advance social justice. She became an early leader in the original Black Panther Party in 1967, and in 1970 collaborated with her late husband Eldridge Cleaver to establish the Black Panthers' International Section in Algeria. She is on the faculty at Emory Law School, and has published work in numerous books, magazines, and newspapers. She is a co-editor, with George Katsiaficas, of *Liberation, Imagination, and the Black Panther Party* and the editor of Eldridge Cleaver's *Target Zero: A Life in Writing.* Cleaver has appeared in numerous documentary films, most recently *Black Panthers: Vanguard of the Revolution,* directed by Stanley Nelson.

Sylviane A. Diouf is an award-winning historian of the African Diaspora. She is the author of eleven books, including *Slavery's Exiles: The Story of the American Maroons, Servants of Allah: African Muslims Enslaved in the Americas,* and *Dreams of Africa in Alabama: The Slave Ship Clotilda and the Story of the Last Africans Brought to America,* and the editor of *Fighting the Slave Trade: West African Strategies.* Diouf is the director of the Lapidus Center for the Historical Analysis of Transatlantic Slavery and a curator at the Schomburg Center for Research in Black Culture.

Emory Douglas created the visual identity for the Black Panther Party, and his iconic images came to symbolize the struggles of the movement. As the Party's revolutionary artist and minister of culture from 1967 until the 1980s, Douglas's work, described as "Militant Chic," featured in most issues of the newspaper the *Black Panther.* His work was characterized by strong graphic images of young African American men, women, and children. Douglas continues to create art with social and political concerns transcending borders.

Ericka Huggins is an educator, Black Panther Party member, former political prisoner,

CONTRIBUTOR BIOGRAPHIES

human rights activist, and poet. For thirty-five years Huggins has lectured in the United States and internationally on human rights, restorative justice and, the role of spiritual practice in sustaining activism and promoting social change.

Michael James was born in New York and grew up in Connecticut but has lived in Chicago for fifty-five years. A longtime political activist and community organizer, James is also an actor, writer, and photographer. He encourages everyone to do good in the world.

Jose (Cha Cha) Jimenez was born in Puerto Rico and grew up in the barrio on the Northside of Chicago. He joined gangs, and after several bouts in jails became president of the Young Lords gang until he finally turned his life around and transformed the Young Lords into the Young Lords Organization, a human rights movement for self-determination.

Peniel E. Joseph is founding director of the Center for the Study of Race and Democracy and a professor of history at Tufts University. He is the author of *Waiting 'Til the Midnight Hour: A Narrative History of Black Power in America; Dark Days, Bright Nights: From Black Power to Barack Obama;* and *Stokely: A Life.* He is the editor of *The Black Power Movement: Rethinking the Civil Rights-Black Power Era* and *Neighborhood Rebels: Black Power at the Local Level.*

Maulana Karenga is professor and chair of the Department of Africana Studies, California State University, Long Beach. He is the creator of the pan-African and African American holiday Kwanzaa and of Nguzo Saba, the official Kwanzaa website. Karenga

is the chair of the social change organization Us and the author of *Kawaida and Questions of Life and Struggle.*

Khalil Gibran Muhammad is a visiting professor of history at the CUNY Graduate Center and the director of the Schomburg Center for Research in Black Culture, the New York Public Library. He is the author of *The Condemnation of Blackness: Race, Crime, and the Making of Modern Urban America,* which won the 2011 John Hope Franklin Publication Prize in American studies; a contributing author of a 2014 National Research Council study, *The Growth of Incarceration in the United States: Exploring Causes and Consequences,* and co-editor of a special issue, "Constructing the Carceral State," of the *Journal of American History.*

Jeffrey O.G. Ogbar is a professor of history and the founding director of the Center for the Study of Popular Music. He is the author of *Black Power: Radical Politics and African American Identity* and *Hip-Hop Revolution: The Culture and Politics of Rap* and the editor of other several books, including *The Harlem Renaissance Revisited: Politics, Arts, and Letters.* Raised in Los Angeles, California, Ogbar received his BA in history from Morehouse College and his MA and PhD in history from Indiana University.

Brenda Gayle Plummer has a joint appointment in the departments of History and Afro-American Studies at the University of Wisconsin, Madison. Her research focus is the history of U.S. foreign relations, African American history, and Caribbean history. She is the author, notably, of *In Search of Power: African Americans in the Era of Decolonization, 1956–1974* and *Rising Wind: Black Americans and U.S. Foreign Affairs, 1935–1960* and the editor of *Window on Freedom: Race, Civil Rights, and Foreign Affairs, 1945–1988.*

Russell Rickford, an assistant professor of history at Cornell University, teaches and writes about the Black Radical Tradition. He is the author of *We Are an African People: Black Power and Independent Education from 1965,* and *Betty Shabazz: Surviving Malcolm X.* He is the editor of *Beyond Boundaries: The Manning Marable Reader,* and the co-author of *Spoken Soul: The Story of Black English.*

James Edward Smethurst, a professor of Afro-American studies at the University of Massachusetts, Amherst, is the author of *The New Red Negro: The Literary Left and African American Poetry, 1930–1946; The Black Arts Movement;* and *The African American Roots of Modernism.* He is also the co-editor of *Left of the Color Line, Radicalism in the South Since Reconstruction,* and *SOS—Calling All Black People: A Black Arts Movement Reader.*

Jakobi Williams is an associate professor in the Department of African American and African Diaspora Studies and the Department of History at Indiana University. His most recent book, *From the Bullet to the Ballot: The Illinois Chapter of the Black Panther Party and Racial Coalition Politics in Chicago,* was published by the University of North Carolina Press under its John Hope Franklin Series.

Komozi Woodard is a professor of history, public policy, and Africana studies at Sarah Lawrence College. He began as managing editor of the *Black Newark* newspaper and radio program in the Black Power movement and as editor of the *Main Trend* cultural journal in the Black Arts Movement. He is the author of *A Nation Within a Nation: Amiri Baraka (LeRoi Jones) and Black Power Politics* and *The Making of*

the New Ark; editor of *The Black Power Movement: Amiri Baraka from Black Arts to Black Radicalism;* and co-editor of *Freedom North, Groundwork,* and *Want to Start a Revolution?: Radical Women in the Black Freedom Struggle.*

NOTES

CHAPTER 2. The Black Power Movement, the Black Panther Party, and Racial Coalitions

1. Laura Pulido, *Black, Brown, Yellow, and Left: Radical Activism in Los Angeles* (Berkeley: University of California Press, 2006), 167–168.

2. Jeffrey O.G. Ogbar, *Black Power: Radical Politics and African American Identity* (Baltimore, MD: Johns Hopkins University Press, 2004), 172–173.

3. Pulido, *Black, Brown, Yellow, and Left,* 109–110.

4. Hank "Poison" Gaddis, interview by author, May 17, 2008. Gaddis served as security/organizer under Bob Lee during his tenure as a member of the Illinois Black Panther Party.

5. Yvonne King, presentation on the Illinois Black Panther Party, Fortieth Reunion of the Black Panther Party, Oakland, California, Oct. 13, 2007, audio and video files in possession of author; Robert (Bob) E. Lee, interview by author, Oct. 22, 2008. King served as a field secretary and organizer for the Rainbow Coalition and later was appointed deputy minister of labor for the Illinois Black Panther Party. Lee was a member of the Illinois Black Panther Party from the fall of 1968 to May of 1970.

6. Charles E. Jones, "Arm Yourself or Harm Yourself: People's Party II and the Black Panther Party in Houston, Texas," in *On the Ground: The Black Panther Party in Communities Across America,* ed. Judson Jeffries (Jackson: University Press of Mississippi, 2010), 3–40.

7. Ogbar, *Black Power,* 176–177.

8. Ibid., 172–173.

9. Johanna Fernandez, "Between Social Service Reform and Revolutionary Politics: The Young Lords, Late Sixties Radicalism, and Community Organizing in New York City" in *Freedom North: Black Freedom Struggles Outside the South, 1940–1980,* eds. Jeanne Theoharis and Komozi Woodard (New York: Palgrave, 2003), 255–285.

10. "United Front Against Fascism Conference," July 19, 1969, Box 229, Folder 4, Item 1, p. 9, Red Squad papers, Chicago History Museum, Chicago, Illinois. Bill Knustler was the preeminent movement lawyer out of New York. He participated in the Chicago Eight conspiracy trial. Ron Dellums later served as a U.S. congressman and mayor of Oakland, California.

11. Joshua Bloom and Waldo Martin, *Black Against Empire: The History and Politics of the Black Panther Party* (Berkeley: University of California Press, 2012), 301–302.

12. George Katsiaficas, "Organization and Movements: The Case of the Black Panther Party and the Revolutionary People's Constitutional Convention of 1970," in *Liberation, Imagination, and the Black Panther Party,* eds. Kathleen Cleaver and George Katsiaficas (New York: Routledge, 2001) 149.

CHAPTER 3. Black Power and "Education for Liberation"

1. Steven Hahn, *A Nation Under Our Feet: Black Political Struggles in the Rural South, from Slavery to the Great Migration* (Cambridge, MA: Belknap Press of Harvard University, 2003), 23; Manning Marable, *Race, Reform, and Rebellion: The Second Reconstruction and Beyond in Black America, 1945–2006* (Jackson: University of Mississippi, 2007), 59–74.

2. Clarence Taylor, *Knocking at Our Own Door: Milton Galamison and the Struggle to Integrate New York City Schools* (New York: Columbia University Press, 1997); "The Silent Disaster," *Washington Post,* April 18, 1967, A12.

3. Jim Leeson, "Theme and Variations," *Southern Education Report,* July–August (1968): 6.

4. Thomas J. Sugrue, *Sweet Land of Liberty: The Forgotten Struggle for Civil Rights in the North* (New York: Random House, 2009), 451–592; Russell Rickford, "Integration, Black Nationalism, and Radical Democratic Transformation in African American Philosophies of Education, 1965–1974," in *The New Black History: Revisiting the Second Reconstruction,* eds. Manning Marable and Elizabeth Kai Hinton (New York: Palgrave Macmillan, 2013), 287–318; Grace Lee Boggs, "Towards a New System of Education," *Foresight,* October 1968.

5. "Resolutions: Negro Teachers' Association's Conference," 1967 pamphlet, Box 24, Folder 8, United Federation of Teachers Collection, Tamiment Library and Robert F. Wagner Labor Archives, New York University.

6. Martha Biondi, *The Black Revolution on Campus* (Berkeley: University of California Press, 2012); Lerone Bennett Jr. "Confrontation on the Campus," *Ebony,* May 1968, 29.

7. *Ibid.,* 28.

8. James Turner, "Black Studies and a Black Philosophy of Education," *Black Lines,* Winter 1970, 6; Ibram Rogers, "Celebrating 40 Years of Activism," *Diverse Issues in Higher Education,* June 29, 2006, 20.

9. Henry Hampton and Steve Fayer, eds., *Voices of Freedom: An Oral History of the Civil Rights Movement from the 1950s through the 1980s* (New York: Bantam, 1990), 446; Keith Lowe, "Towards a Black University," *Liberator,* September 1968, 4–9; Vincent Harding, "Toward the Black University," *Ebony,* August 1970, 156–159.

10. Matthew J. Countryman, *Up South: Civil Rights and Black Power in Philadelphia* (Philadelphia: University of Pennsylvania Press, 2006), 223–257; "Carolina Negroes Ask School Power," *New York Times,* January 29, 1968, 40.

11. Inner City Parents Council, "Detroit Schools—A Blueprint for Change," *Liberator,* September 1967, 9; see, for example, Nathan Hare, "Bourgeois Teachers in Black Schools," *Liberator,* March 1967, 6; Charles V. Hamilton, "Education in the Black Community: An Examination of the Realities," *Freedomways,* Fall 1968, 320; Toni Cade, "The Children Who Get Cheated," *Redbook,* January 1970; June Jordan, *His Own Where* (New York: Crowell, 1971).

12. Daniel Perlstein, *Justice, Justice: School Politics and the Eclipse of Liberalism* (New York: Peter Lang, 2004); Preston Wilcox, "Changing Conceptions of Community," *Educational Leadership,* May 1972, 681; "Ocean Hill Target for Black Militants," *New York Amsterdam News,* March 22, 1969.

13. Dada Folayan and Ndugu Charles Robinson, "Shule Ya Uhuru: Freedom and Manhood," and Ndugu Mamadou Lumumba, "Philosophy of Freedom School (Shule Ya Uhuru) Part 3: An Administrator's View," in *High School,* eds. Ronald Gross and Paul Osterman (New York: Simon & Shuster, 1971), 285–292, 300.

14. Angela Davis, *Angela Davis: An Autobiography* (New York: International Publishers, 1974), 181–183.

NOTES

15. Charlayne Hunter, "Panthers Indoctrinate the Young," *The New York Times,* August 18, 1969, 31; "Liberation Means Freedom," *Black Panther,* July 5, 1969, 3; "Liberation School," *Black Panther,* August 16, 1969, 14; JoNina M. Abron, "'Serving the People': The Survival Programs of the Black Panther Party," in *The Black Panther Party Reconsidered,* ed. Charles E. Jones (Baltimore, MD: Black Classic Press, 1998), 177–192; Eldridge Cleaver, "Education and Revolution," *Black Scholar,* November 1969, 47.

16. "Mecca for Blackness," *Ebony,* May 1970, 96–98.

17. California Association for Afro-American Education and Nairobi College, "The Independent Black Institution," In *African Congress: A Documentary of the First Modern Pan-African Congress,* ed. Amiri Baraka (New York: William Morrow & Company, 1972), 285.

18. Peniel E. Joseph, "Introduction: Toward a Historiography of the Black Power Movement," in *The Black Power Movement: Rethinking the Civil Rights-Black Power Era,* ed. Joseph (New York: Routledge, 2006), 7.

19. Institute for African Education pamphlet, Box 7, Sixth Pan-African Congress Collection, Moorland-Spingarn Research Center, Howard University; Jitu Weusi, "Around Our Way," *Black News,* April 4, 1973, 18; "Council of Independent Black Institutions: Summary from 1st Work Meeting," 1972 pamphlet, Labadie Pamphlets, Special Collections, University of Michigan.

20. "Elimu Ya Kujitegemea," Shule Ya Watoto newsletter, c. 1972, Box 18, Preston Wilcox Papers, Schomburg Center.

21. Paulo Freire, *Pedagogy in Process: The Letters to Guinea-Bissau* (New York: Seabury Press, 1978), 15.

22. Doxey Wilkerson, "Inequalities in Education and Powerlessness," 1974 pamphlet, Box 17, Folder 8, Doxey Wilkerson Papers, Schomburg Center.

Chapter 4. America Means Prison: Political Prisoners in the Age of Black Power

1. Much of the work for this chapter builds on Dan Berger, *Captive Nation: Black Prison Organizing in the Civil Rights Era* (Chapel Hill: University of North Carolina Press, 2014). More detailed description of key cases and a substantive bibliography can be found there.

2. Joshua Bloom and Waldo Martin Jr., *Black Against Empire: The History and Politics of the Black Panther Party* (Berkeley: University of California Press, 2012), 70–71.

3. Donna Murch, *Living for the City: Education, Migration, and the Rise of the Black Panther Party in Oakland, California* (Chapel Hill: University of North Carolina Press, 2010).

4. Rebecca N. Hill, *Men, Mobs, and Law: Anti-Lynching and Labor Defense in US Radical History* (Durham, NC: Duke University Press, 2009); Peniel E. Joseph, *Waiting 'Til the Midnight Hour: A Narrative History of Black Power* (New York: Henry Holt, 2006).

5. George L Jackson, *Soledad Brother: The Prison Letters of George Jackson* (Chicago: Lawrence Hill Books, 1994 [1970]), 26.

6. Danielle L. McGuire, *At the Dark End of the Street* (New York: Alfred A. Knopf, 2010), 202–228.

7. For a brief survey on these and other cases, see Dan Berger, *The Struggle Within: Prisons, Political Prisoners, and Mass Movements in the United States* (Oakland, CA: PM Press, 2014).

8. A small sampling of the literature on the dramatic expansion of U.S. prisons includes Ruth Wilson Gilmore, *Golden Gulag: Prisons, Surplus, Crisis, and Opposition in Globalizing California* (Berkeley: University of California Press, 2007); Marie Gottschalk, *The Prison and the Gallows* (New York: Cambridge University Press, 2006); Berger, *Captive Nation.*

9. Beth E. Richie, *Arrested Justice: Black Women, Violence, and America's Prison Nation* (New York: NYU Press, 2012).

Chapter 5. The Black Arts Movement

1. Malcolm X, "Speech on the Founding of the OAAU, June 28, 1964." http://www.thinking-together.org/rcream/archive/Old/S2006/comp/OAAU.pdf.

2. *Ibid.*

3. Baraka, *The Autobiography of LeRoi Jones/Amiri Baraka* (New York: Freundlich Books, 1983): 181–182.

Chapter 6 Testimony (Kathleen Neal Cleaver): Art and Revolution

1. *Cinema and the Racial Imaginary held at the Whitechapel Gallery,* 7 June–4 September 2005. Courtesy Whitechapel Gallery, Whitechapel Gallery Archive.

2. Eric Pace, "African Nations Open 12-Day Cultural Festival with Parade Through Algiers," *New York Times,* July 22, 1969, 9.

3. Eric Pace, "Cleaver Assails Apollo Program," *New York Times,* July 21, 1969, 40.

Chapter 6. International Dimensions of the Black Power Movement

1. Cedric J. Robinson, *Black Marxism: The Making of the Black Radical Tradition,* rep. (Chapel Hill: University of North Carolina Press, 2000); Robin D.J. Kelley, *Freedom Dreams: The Black Radical Imagination* (Boston: Beacon Press, 2002); Reiland Rabaka, *Africana Critical Theory: Reconstructing the Black Radical Tradition, from W.E.B. Du Bois and C.L.R. James to Frantz Fanon and Amilcar Cabral* (Lanham, MD: Lexington Books, 2010).

2. Yohuru R. Williams, "American-Exported Black Nationalism: The Student Nonviolent Coordinating Committee, the Black Panther Party, and the Worldwide Freedom Struggle, 1967–1972," *Negro History Bulletin* 60 (July–Sept. 1997): 13. See also Brenda Gayle Plummer, *In Search of Power: African Americans in the Age of Decolonization, 1956–1974* (New York and London: Cambridge University Press, 2013).

3. Michael J. Shapiro, "Moral geographies and the ethics of post-sovereignty," *Public Culture* 6.3 (1994): 481.

4. For Malcolm X's internationalism, see especially, David Gallen, ed., *Malcolm X: The FBI File* (New York: Caroll & Graf, 1991); Manning Marable, *Malcolm X: A Life of Reinvention* (New York: Viking, 2011); Ruby Essien-Udom and E.U. Essien-Udom, "Malcolm X: An International Man," in *Malcolm X, the Man and His Times,* ed. John Henrik Clark (New York: Macmillan, 1969), 235–267.

5. Fanon Che Wilkins, "SNCC and Africa Before the Launching of Black Power, 1960–1965," *Journal of African American History* 92 (Winter 2007): 469.

6. John Lewis, *Walking with the Wind: A Memoir of the Movement* (New York: Simon and Schuster, 1998), 295 (emphasis in original).

7. For Black Power in Canada see David Austin, *Fear of a Black Nation: Race, Sex,*

and Security in Sixties Montreal (Toronto: Between the Lines, 2013); Jennifer B. Smith, *An International History of the Black Panther Party* (New York: Garland, 1999); Steve Hewitt, *Spying 101: The RCMP's Secret Activities at Canadian Universities, 1917–1997* (Toronto: University of Toronto Press, 2002).

8. *The Black Power Revolution of 1970: A Retrospective,* ed. Selwyn Ryan and Taimoon Stewart with Roy McCree (St. Augustine, Trinidad: I.S.E.R., University of the West Indies Press, 1995); Brian Meeks, *Radical Caribbean: From Black Power to Abu Bakr* (Barbados: University of the West Indies Press, 1996); Maurice St. Pierre, "Diasporan Intellectuals in Post Independent Guyana, Jamaica, and Trinidad and Tobago: A Generational Analysis," *Souls* 10, no. 2 (2008): 138–154.

9. For the Black Panther Party of Israel, see Oz Frankel, "The Black Panthers of Israel and the Politics of the Radical Analogy," in *Black Power Beyond Borders: The Global Dimensions of the Black Power Movement,* ed. Nico Slate (New York: Palgrave Macmillan, 2012), 81–106; Deborah Bernstein, "The Black Panthers of Israel 1971–1972: Contradictions and Protest in the Process of Nation-Building," Ph.D. dissertation, University of Sussex, 1976.

10. B.R. Ambedkar, "Castes in India, Their Origin and Development," *The Essential Writings of B.R. Ambedkar,* ed. Valerian Rodrigues (New Delhi: Oxford University Press, 2002), 261.

11. For the Dalit Panthers, see Prashad, Vijay. "Afro-Dalits of the Earth, Unite!" *African Studies Review* 43, no. 1 (2000): 189–201; Nico Slate, "The Dalit Panthers: Race, Caste, and Black Power in India," in *Black Power Beyond Borders,* 127–145.

12. For Black Power in Australia and New Zealand, see Roberta B. Sykes, *Black Power in Australia* (South Yarra, Vic., Australia: Heinemann Educational Australia, 1975); Rhonda Y. Williams, *Concrete Demands: The Search for Black Power in the 20th Century* (New York and London: Routledge, 2015); Robbie Shilliam, "The Polynesian Panthers and the Black Power Gang: Surviving Racism and Colonialism in Aotearoa Press, New Zealand," in *Black Power Beyond Borders,* 107–126.